MW01172270

FIVE TOUGH TALKS

HOW TO LEAD BRAVE CONVERSATIONS FOR EXCEPTIONAL RESULTS

NICOLE M. BIANCHI

Cover Design by Kelly Laine Design

ISBN: 979-8-9885808-0-5 (paperback edition)
ISBN: 979-8-9885808-1-2 (hardback edition)

Coraggio Publishers

Five Tough Talks: How to Lead Brave Conversations for
Exceptional Results

By Nicole M. Bianchi

"Every leader wrestles with having difficult conversations and this book provides a 'user's manual' to help navigate, rather than avoid, these essential conversations. We can't simplify other human beings, but we can improve how efficiently and effectively we work with others. Bianchi's practical advice will help leaders learn how to engage in any/all conversations, no matter how challenging."

DANIELLE KIRGAN, CHIEF
TRANSFORMATION AND HR
OFFICER, MACY'S, INC.

"Nicole does it again with Tough Talks. The small brave move of having a tough conversation is essential for healthy, substantial relationships, both personal and professional. The pages are full of practical steps with personal stories that bring to life the possibilities in your own tough conversations."

DENICE BIOCCA, CHRO GAS POWER,
GE VERNOVA

"Nicole does it again, with bravership, providing a handbook for not avoiding tough conversations and providing actionable suggestions within the capacity of everyone regardless of position or title. The worst tough talk is the one you don't have, and Nicole offers personable, refreshing, and inspiring examples along with step-by-step guides to doing what you might imagine you cannot do. Written in a way that makes you think that Nicole is right by your side, both coaching and encouraging you every step of the way."

BARRY POSNER, PH.D., CO-AUTHOR
OF *THE LEADERSHIP CHALLENGE*
AND *A LEADER'S LEGACY*

"Having spent most of my career as a successful 'turn around' leader, I have had more than my share of tough conversations. They were always the hardest part of leadership for me and they never got easier. I wish I had Nicole's book earlier in my career. It would have saved me restless nights and prevented some damaged relationships."

DEAN HOLLIS, FOUNDER AND CEO
OF DIVENTURES

"How many times in life have you completed a difficult task and said to yourself, 'Phew! That wasn't so bad after all.' What Nicole provides for all readers is the blueprint to be able to go into any situation with the mindset of, 'I'm ready! This isn't going to be too difficult!'"

PERCY E. FIELDS III, PRESIDENT & GENERAL MANAGER, BELT RAILWAY COMPANY OF CHICAGO

"Being intentional about how to look the necessary conversations in the face and proceed with confidence is at the heart of *Five Tough Talks*. When employees master the five levels they will undoubtedly unlock new levels of possibility, partnership, and performance inside their organizations and help make the world a great place to work."

GREG HONEY, EVP & CHRO FARM CREDIT CANADA

"Tough conversations are a necessary part of good leadership. Nicole brilliantly provides a straightforward guide to making these conversations less daunting and more effective. *Five Tough Talks* is the playbook that every new and seasoned leader needs in their toolkit."

PATRICIA KEARNS, PRESIDENT & CEO, QLI

"In *Five Tough Talks,* Nicole Bianchi has created a clear playbook for leaders who want to become stellar communicators. Packed with scripts, questions, and tactics, this is a book readers will turn to again and again to lead more confidently, handle delicate situations, and drive results."

JOE MULL, AUTHOR OF *EMPLOYALTY: HOW TO IGNITE COMMITMENT AND KEEP TOP TALENT IN THE NEW AGE OF WORK*

"*Five Tough Talks* has great advice for all. I could have used a copy during my lengthy journalism career and years teaching journalism. I'm sure it will help resolve many potential conflicts!"

DARREL JANZ, ONE OF CANADA'S
MOST NOTABLE JOURNALISTS WITH
OVER 50 YEARS AT CTV NEWS
CANADA

To my dad

Richard Dean Giese, The Sarpy County Farmer.
A business leader who knew when and how to
have tough conversations. This skill enabled him to
achieve exceptional results in life and in business.
The power of regret is in part why this book was
written. I wish I had known at 28 years old how to
have the Moving On conversation before my dad died of
cancer at age 52. I love and miss you every day, Dad.

To the leaders

who continually tossed me into the toughest
conversations of my life, coaching me along the way
knowing I would learn and grow exponentially from
each of these moments. Thank you for believing in me.

To YOU

who is reading this and wants to grow and be better at
having tough conversations. This book,
the framework, and the tools are for you.
Now, let's get to work.

CONTENTS

Introduction   xiii

1. The Five Types of Tough Talks   1
2. How We Work   17
3. The Ask   39
4. What's Going On?   53
5. Being Better   69
6. Moving On   83
7. The Tough Talk Process   97
8. Protect Your Energy   115
9. Leading Brave Conversations   129

Conclusion   141
You Don't Have to Go It Alone   149
Selected References   153
Acknowledgments   157
About the Author   161

INTRODUCTION

Nobody likes having a tough talk. They are uncomfortable, awkward, and often heated. Yet, they are necessary in your personal and professional life. It is time for a tough conversation about tough conversations. In all honesty, you are probably terrible at them. The reason you are not good at tough conversations is because you don't practice them, which is the result of not knowing *how* to do them.

Tough talks are necessary to elicit change and must be impactful to achieve results. What stops you from having the conversation is fear: How will my conversation be received? Can I make it clear and concise? Will it make sense? Will I be able to act on the promises made? How will the conversation affect others? Will the conversation lead to a change for the better or will it be worse?

The fear of regret is paralyzing. If you've had a tough talk that didn't achieve the result you needed, it's easy to assume you will have the same outcome again. But the fear of regret should outweigh the fear of not having the conversation. It's okay to fear a difficult conversation. All you need are the tools and practice to help work through that fear.

Think of the opportunities you might be missing by not having that conversation. When you make assumptions and allow conversations to sit and swirl in your head, you waste time. Wasted time leads to more wasted time, and timeliness is critical when you need to lead a tough conversation, otherwise you risk weakening its impact. Tough talks must happen when they arise. Michael Bungay Stanier, author of *The Coaching Habit,* uses the analogy that waiting to have a tough conversation is like letting a stain set in to your laundry:

> **"If you wait too long, the stain sets, and even with treatments, it never quite goes away. If you have an inkling you should have a conversation, it probably means you should have the conversation—not, 'I wonder if I should have had a conversation.' Treat the stain early."**

Leaders who aren't able to have difficult conversations sometimes ask someone else in their organization or hire a consultant to have the conversation for them. Unfortunately, this does not serve anybody well, especially the leader. You need to learn how to embrace tough conversations so that you are not only more effective but exceptional in your role.

You are probably familiar with the "feedback sandwich:"

- Start the conversation with a positive comment
- Add the critical component
- Finish the conversation with a positive comment

You should *never* use the feedback sandwich during a tough conversation. It diminishes the impact and results you are trying to achieve. Provide positive feedback as part of your daily routine so that when it's time to lead a tough conversation, you can focus on the key message and align on the desired outcome.

As an executive for 16 years with two Fortune 300 companies, I have had countless tough talks. Over the last 11 years as an executive coach, one of the reasons I'm hired is to work with individuals whose leaders have decided they need to perform better. What those individuals really needed was for their leader to have had a tough conversation with them months earlier. It would have prevented the need to bring me in as a consultant in the first place.

Now my focus is teaching leaders how to turn a tough talk into a brave conversation. I help them understand each type of conversation and how to prepare, practice, and process before and after. The results are greater confidence, productivity, and a greater impact on the team and the organization.

If you are a leader who struggles or avoids difficult conversations, this will become your playbook for every tough talk you need to have in your professional and personal life.

There are five types of tough talks:

1. **How We Work.** During this conversation, a leader intentionally makes an agreement for how to best work together. They state their expectations and ask what is expected of them. The parties align on the rules, routines, and rhythms needed to work together and perform at their best. It sounds like an easy conversation to have, but unfortunately most leaders skip this foundational step.

2. **The Ask.** During this conversation, a leader acknowledges they need something from the other person. It could be clarity on priorities, a specific form of help, or a request to be a mentor. Leaders are considered experts, so it can be difficult for them to ask for something even when it is necessary.

3. **What's Going On?** This conversation is an exploration into a change or shift in someone's behavior, performance, or relationship. It usually occurs in one area, such as routinely arriving late for work or no longer responding to messages. When you notice a change in a particular behavior, don't ignore it—take the time to be curious about what's going on by having this conversation.

4. **Being Better.** This conversation confronts an issue related to behavior or performance that has become a pattern. As a leader, you need to shine a light on the issue and guide the person out of the situation so they can become better.

5. **Moving On.** This conversation acknowledges that things aren't working and you must determine a new path forward. This is the toughest conversation to have because it is always a departure conversation —not necessarily a departure from the

company but more often a departure from either a position, project, or relationship.

The How We Work, The Ask, and What's Going On? conversations are easier to have than the Being Better and Moving On conversations. I'm going to help you become comfortable with the first three, because when you invest time in those conversations, the other two will be easier and less frequent.

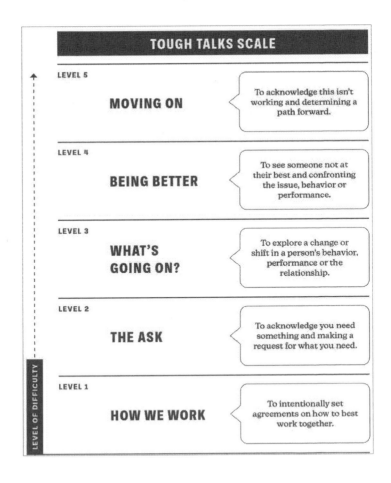

TOUGH TALKS SCALE

LEVEL OF DIFFICULTY

LEVEL 5
MOVING ON
To acknowledge this isn't working and determining a path forward.

LEVEL 4
BEING BETTER
To see someone not at their best and confronting the issue, behavior or performance.

LEVEL 3
WHAT'S GOING ON?
To explore a change or shift in a person's behavior, performance or the relationship.

LEVEL 2
THE ASK
To acknowledge you need something and making a request for what you need.

LEVEL 1
HOW WE WORK
To intentionally set agreements on how to best work together.

I will teach you how to prepare for a tough talk, what to do in the messy middle, how to pivot if it doesn't go well, and how to end each conversation with accountability and direction to drive the change you need.

Bolder conversations equal stronger connections. If you are unsure whether you need to have a tough conversation, Lara Abrash, Chair for the Board of Directors at Deloitte US suggests that leaders ask themselves:

> **"Is this a tough conversation I need to have, or is it for someone else to have? Does it require immediate attention? Does it require me to lean in? Does it need my voice?"**

Bravery is a skill and leadership is an action. I will help you develop the skills so you can lead the conversations with bravery and achieve exceptional results.

1

THE FIVE TYPES OF TOUGH TALKS

AS A LEADER, you know you need to have the tough talks. You have probably read numerous articles from executive coaches about how difficult conversations are essential for good leadership.

But according to VitalSmarts, a leadership training company, more than 80% of workers procrastinate having a tough conversation, and 1 in 4 people put it off for six months hoping the issue will resolve itself.

Procrastination is a function of not prioritizing the conversation, and it isn't prioritized because people lack confidence in their skills. Most people haven't developed the skills necessary for having a tough talk because they are afraid of conflict.

According to Dr. Charles Fay, President of the Love and Logic Institute, conflict avoidance can be traced to your childhood:

"Part of the reason involves the fact that many of us, when we were children, failed to learn what healthy, loving, and respectful relationships look like. Although most of our parents did their very best, many of them struggled with learning these lessons as well."

Parents avoid conflict, workers avoid conflict, leaders avoid conflict, and everyone suffers as a result. People don't like feeling uncomfortable, being perceived as unkind, or not pleasing others. I am a recovering people-pleaser who doesn't like feeling uncomfortable or making others uncomfortable.

Luckily, early in my career I had a mentor who pushed me outside my comfort zone. Whenever I shared a difficult situation, he'd take time to coach me and think about the conversation I needed to have. Then he'd encourage me to have a tough talk and held me accountable by insisting I report back to him afterward. That accountability prevented me from procrastinating and avoiding the conflict.

When you avoid conflict, it signals to the other person that you accept their problematic behavior and they can't trust you to be honest with them.

You teach others how to treat you by:

- **What you allow**
- **What you reject**
- **What you reinforce**

Having tough conversations is the best way to build a trusted, respectful relationship. Daniel Coyle, author of *The Culture Code: The Secrets of Highly Successful Groups*, explains:

> **"Group culture is one of the most powerful forces on the planet. Culture is a set of living relationships working toward a shared goal. It's not something you are. It's something you do."**

The three group skills needed for an effective organization are to build safety, share vulnerability, and establish purpose. When you create trust, belonging, and a sense of vulnerability, having tough conversations becomes easier over time.

But in the beginning, they can be awkward, messy, and uncomfortable. Take the following self-assessment to find out how comfortable you currently are with having a tough talk:

Rate yourself on FREQUENCY:

How frequently do you have these tough talks?

1 Never
2 Rarely
3 Sometimes
4 Usually
5 Always

TOUGH TALK TYPE	FREQUENCY
MOVING ON	
BEING BETTER	
WHAT'S GOING ON?	
THE ASK	
HOW WE WORK	

Rate yourself on CONFIDENCE:

How confident are you in having these tough talks?

1 Not confident
2 Slightly
3 Somewhat
4 Fairly
5 Very confident

TOUGH TALK TYPE	CONFIDENCE
MOVING ON	
BEING BETTER	
WHAT'S GOING ON?	
THE ASK	
HOW WE WORK	

After you complete the self-assessment, answer these questions:

1. Which is the toughest for you?
2. Why do you think so?
3. What do you notice between frequency and confidence?

Early in my career I was hired as a human resources (HR) manager. Prior to starting the position, the company conducted an employee survey about HR. One of the employee comments was, "Going to HR is like getting an enema." That was tough feedback to hear.

My job was to change that perception and their relationship with HR leadership. I was young, inexperienced, and thought I could influence them, but most of the employees had been working there more than 15 years. One employee was particularly difficult, and I was tasked with having a tough conversation with her.

I didn't prepare prior to the meeting, and the employee was immediately defensive. Nobody at the company had ever had a tough talk with her, so she didn't think her behavior was a problem.

I was shocked at her response and resorted to conflict avoidance. I stumbled through the conversation and did not accomplish my goal. That conversation caused more disruption rather than the necessary change. She continued to be difficult to work with, but the conversation was a starting point.

An example from my personal life is from a recent trip my husband and I took to Italy. We were in Sicily, and locals were jumping off an old stone fort wall into the ocean. My husband wanted us to jump, so we approached the edge of the wall. It was very high up and I'm afraid of heights, so I just peered over the edge, looking down.

The locals began cheering, "You can do it, Miss! You can do it!" They counted down three, two, one, but I couldn't jump. I was too scared. After continued chanting, cheering, and counting down, I finally took a deep breath and jumped. I screamed like a child the entire way down. I hit the water with a slap and came up coughing and sputtering with water up my nose and in my mouth.

Embarrassed, I swam to the rope ladder, climbed up the wall, and peered over the edge again. More locals had gathered, and another tourist joined me. She was scared, and I offered words of encouragement. Now the crowd cheered for both of us to jump. When she refused, I heard, "Miss, jump again!"

This time when I jumped, I didn't scream. I still hit the water with an ugly splash, but at least I improved. And on my third and final jump, I got playful and stretched my arms and legs in a wide V shape.

The reason I jumped several times wasn't to achieve perfection, it was to get a little better each time I tried. Frequency builds confidence. I became a little less fearful. It's like having tough conversations. The more time you invest in them, the more confident you become until tough talks become the new way of doing things.

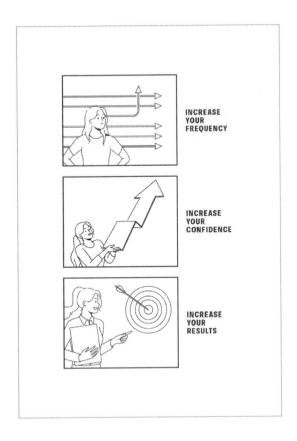

1. How We Work

As I've mentioned, each type of talk is a little tougher than the previous one. The How We Work conversation is the easiest of the five to embrace and the foundation for establishing good communication. Yet, many leaders—especially those new to a leadership role—skip this important conversation. It is often unintentional; they become too busy and assume their team knows what is expected of them, which is a mistake.

Jane Anders, Senior Vice President - Asia Pacific Innovation, R&D, Product Development & Packaging Development at Estée Lauder offers this advice:

> **"The longer you let it fester, the tougher it will be. The more you do it, the easier it gets. Prep and invest the time. Think through how to open the conversation. What are the possible reactions? It's really important you are fair and look at it from all sides. Remember, we hire smart people who want to do a good job."**

Leaders become so focused on goals or objectives —*what* they need to deliver—that they forget to invest in the *how*. The How We Work conversation designs the rules, routines, and rhythms for success.

It allows a leader to outline expectations, ask for what they need from their team, and allow team members to ask for what they need from the leader in return.

The How We Work conversation is one of the most important that leaders can have when being promoted from a peer to a manager position. They need to reset boundaries and consider which agreements will be most important in their new role with their team. I was asked to coach a leader who had been in her peer-to-manager role for six months, and she was struggling to manage her team of former co-workers.

One team member was having a performance issue. To maintain an artificial harmony with the employee, the leader took over some of the work the employee wasn't doing.

Unfortunately, because the leader never had the How We Work conversation in the beginning, the problem escalated to a Being Better conversation, which was much more intimidating. The good news is, it is never too late to go back and have the How We Work conversation.

2. The Ask

The next tough talk leaders must have is The Ask. People are hard-wired to be independent, and asking for help feels like relinquishing control. M. Nora

Bouchard, author of *Mayday! Asking for Help in Times of Need* explains:

"We don't want to be ashamed of our situation or come across as incompetent. We make a lot of excuses for not making the request. The irony is that most often, people do want to help."

I coached an emerging, young female leader who wanted a female executive as a mentor. We identified a candidate, but my client assumed the executive was too busy to be a mentor.

She put off having The Ask conversation for 60 days. As a Master Coach, I knew to ask her, "What's the worst that could happen?" My client thought for a moment and responded, "She says no." I simply told her if that happens, we find someone else to ask.

Finally, my client requested that the executive meet for coffee, and she agreed. I coached my client to be clear and concise with her ask.

She wanted the executive to meet with her for 30 minutes once a month to discuss how to navigate projects, approach challenging situations, and to advocate for herself.

Not only did the executive agree to meet monthly, but she wanted to devote an hour to each meeting, and she was grateful she had been asked to be a mentor.

3. What's Going On?

The next type of tough talk is called What's Going On? If you've had the How We Work conversation and established expectations and routines for how you work together, then it's easy to recognize when it's time to have the What's Going On? conversation. You will pick up a cue or clue that something has changed with the person, your relationship, or the work. It can be easy to gloss over the change and assume it will work itself out, but the key is to have this conversation as soon as you notice the change to prevent it from escalating.

I coached a chief executive officer (CEO) who noticed a shift in the relationship between him and his sales manager. The manager was arriving and leaving work on time but no longer putting in extra hours, contributing in meetings, or participating socially at the office.

The CEO assumed that if the manager wanted to share what was going on, he would, and feared that questioning his sales manager would make their relationship worse. This lack of communication contin- ued, and the manager couldn't understand why the

CEO failed to notice that something was wrong and assumed the CEO didn't care. Eventually, the sales manager gave his notice and left the company, which could have been avoided if they had both been brave enough to have the tough conversation.

4. Being Better

The next two types of conversations are tougher because the stakes are higher. The first of those is the Being Better conversation, which requires you to confront an issue related to behavior or performance. Unlike the What's Going On? conversation, this is pointing out that a negative pattern has emerged.

The CEO of a company hired me to work with his leadership team. He said the groups weren't working together or communicating when something impacted another team.

As I gathered feedback from the team, I discovered it was the CEO who needed to be better. His leaders were afraid of having the conversation with him and allowed the issues to continue for too long.

I had to have the Being Better conversation with the CEO and share the feedback from his leaders. He was shocked because nobody had ever had that conversation with him before. Nobody had been brave enough.

He felt exposed and reluctant to admit he needed to change his behavior. I worked with him for a year, coaching him on the How We Work conversation to get him and his leaders back on track.

5. Moving On

The toughest talk to have is Moving On. People assume this is when you fire someone, but that's not always the case. Think of this conversation as a departure from what was, with the goal of moving forward in a position, project, or relationship. You have to let go of what was to move to what should be.

I coached a client who was transitioning into CEO of a company after the previous CEO retired, which would take a year. After four months, the incoming CEO was frustrated because the outgoing CEO did not make any changes. He still came to work every day, and out of habit, his leaders still approached him for direction.

The incoming CEO was not able to set his own direction and vision with the team—the How We Work conversation—with the outgoing CEO still fully immersed. I helped the incoming CEO have the Moving On conversation with the outgoing CEO so they could reshape the transition, move forward faster, and make it work better for everyone.

In the next five chapters, I will explain in detail each type of tough talk, provide examples, and teach you how to effectively lead them. The goal is to develop your confidence and concentrate on the first three conversations so that you have fewer of the last two. By practicing these talks, you move from a position of chance to a position of choice.

Leaving a conversation to chance makes the outcome inconsistent and unreliable. A conversation from a position of choice requires preparation and focus to achieve the desired outcome. Chance is easy, choice is difficult. Don't worry about being perfect. Throughout this process, give yourself grace and permission to experiment. Timothy Ferriss, author of *Tribe of Mentors: Short Life Advice from the Best in the World* says:

> **"Mastery is a journey, not a destination. True masters never believe they have attained mastery. There is always more to be learned and greater skill to be developed."**

Learning how to lead the five tough talks won't happen overnight, but in time, you will gain confidence and lead the conversations with bravery and achieve exceptional results.

2

HOW WE WORK

IN CHAPTER one I shared the story about jumping off the stone wall into the water while on a trip to Italy with my husband. That trip was a six-week tour with several other couples we were friends with as well as people we didn't know.

The first week my husband and I were pulled in different directions trying to accommodate our friends, both old and new. I realized we had been so busy getting ready for the trip we hadn't discussed each other's expectations. I sensed it was time for a How We Work conversation, so I leaned into it.

We talked about what a successful trip looked like for each of us, how much time we wanted to spend one on one, and how much time we wanted to spend with friends and the tour group. Once we agreed on the rules for our trip, we were able to establish routines that allowed us to act on those rules, then check in with each other periodically to make sure we were both still happy with how the trip was progressing.

For example, one rule was to carve out plenty of one-on-one time, so we skipped some of the scheduled tour activities in favor of exploring an area on our own. If we had not had the conversation to ensure we were aligned, we would have spent more time and energy frustrated with each other and the situation. The result was an amazing trip to Italy that also celebrated our 25-year marriage.

Tough Talk: How We Work

As a leader, intentionally setting rules, routines, and rhythms is the most important conversation to have. Unfortunately, many people who are new to leading or new to a position skip this conversation and dive into the work. In a recent poll conducted by Bravium HD, 54% of professionals said they "sometimes" have a How We Work conversation with team members.

Skipping this conversation might not cause an immediate problem, but over time, dysfunction emerges in the form of misunderstanding, lack of clarity, and hurt feelings. Leaders and their team end up wasting time and energy playing defense instead of offense. Phillip K. James, President of WEG Transformers USA, shares:

"You must have the tough conversation. Rarely does it improve by itself naturally, so be a leader. The organization will be negatively affected by you not having the conversation."

It's important to have a clear understanding of each element in the How We Work conversation.

Rules: A set of agreements that are ways to hold each other accountable and are intended to help you deliver on the strategy and goals. Rules outline a set of behaviors that challenge you in new ways.

At Ohio State University, there is a no "C.B.D." rule within its football program—no "complaining, blaming, or defending." When the team meets, if a player makes a C.B.D. comment, another player is required to point it out so the negative talk doesn't persist and infect the rest of the team.

The employee handbook for Nordstrom lists a rule as, "In all things, use your good judgment." At my company, one of our rules is "straight talk," which means having an honest conversation right away.

Routines: These are repeated actions designed to reinforce the behaviors that are most valuable to your team. They are a way of living out the rules, or agreements, you made and help you see the routines in action.

The band Van Halen often included pyrotechnics during their concerts that required extensive safety features from the performance venues. The band's contract was 18 pages. Buried in the contract was a requirement to provide a bowl of M&Ms—with the brown ones removed—in the band's green room.

When the band arrived, if there was a bowl of M&Ms —sans brown ones—they knew the venue had read the entire contract and followed all requirements. If brown M&Ms were present, the band needed to take further action.

I worked with a leader who made a rule to regularly celebrate her team's wins. She created thank you stones and put them on the right side of her desk every Monday morning. Each time she recognized a win and thanked a team member, she moved a stone to the left side of her desk.

I worked with another company that established a rule to insert more energy and fun into their meetings. As they entered the conference room each time, every person clapped slowly at first and then faster and faster, ending with a group high-five as a simple way to gear up for the meeting.

Rhythms: These are how often a leader connects and gains feedback about how well the rules and routines are working. You can't have the How We Work conversation once and then walk away. You need to also agree on how often you will communicate and in what form. Every person is different and will have different needs.

I worked with a CEO who was an empty nester and had a young team at work. She often caught up on emails on the weekends. Even though she never expected her team to respond until Monday, team members thought they had to address her emails right away.

She and her team made an agreement that emails didn't require a response until Monday, and if she had an urgent need on the weekend, she would text instead. This eliminated any weekend work misunderstanding, and everyone knew to check their email first thing every Monday morning.

Another leader I work with takes a proactive approach and includes the following in every email:

Please note: I am sending this email at a time that is convenient for me. Please read and respond at a time that is convenient for you and that fosters a healthy work-life balance.

Setting Intentions

No matter your role in an organization, you need to have the How We Work conversation. It could be leader to direct report, peer to peer, within a project team, or cross disciplinary. The ideal time to have the talk is at the beginning of a new relationship, whether that is a new hire, a new project, a new team, or a new reporting structure.

This conversation provides the foundation for building an effective relationship. I have worked with many well-intended leaders who start off having this conversation only to abandon it over time because they don't revisit the agreements, see the routines in action, or the rhythm doesn't work. When done correctly, How We Work conversations help you proactively solve any problem together. Master Coach Susan Mann shares:

"I think back to becoming a leader in my 20s when a number of the people who reported to me had been my peers and good friends before I was promoted. With the power of rear view vision, I'd be forthright and open in talking about how can we best work together now? What will success look like in our relationship now? What do you want and need from me? What do I want and need from you? I didn't initiate conversations to relaunch our working relationships and to touch base on our friendships as I moved from peer to boss. If I had a do-over, I would make that change."

When everyone knows what is expected of one another, they know how to operate and perform at their best. When you have the conversation early, it proactively fosters good relationships and accelerates performance. The team can anticipate problems, be creative, and take chances together.

When you have the conversation retroactively, it takes more time to repair damaged relationships and realign. Watch any sports team play, and you can immediately see if they are aligned—coaches and players—because it shows in their performance.

Katie Tarman, girls varsity volleyball head coach for Papillion-LaVista South High School in Nebraska, has led her team to three state championship titles in four years. She attributes much of their success to starting each season with the How We Work talk:

"True success in any team situation needs to be peer led, with the leader guiding the team. Each season, I start as if I am a brand new coach and allow the team to organically set the culture for that year. We start the season by asking: What did you love? What did you hate? What do you want us to never let go of? What do we want it to look like this year? What ideas do you have?

"Once they feel the ownership and ability to speak up and ask for what they need, the trust and cohesion begins to build. Then on about day 30 of the season, we make sure each player is communicating what they need. We ask each one to answer: How do you want to be talked to by your team members? What do you want them to talk to you about? How do you want the coaches to talk to you? We

become clear on what each player needs to work best together."

To set intentions during a How We Work conversation, follow these steps:

Step 1: Ask questions. Building relationships and setting intentions won't happen overnight. These agreements require more than one How We Work conversation, especially with one-on-one relationships.

The easiest way to start the conversation is by asking questions. You can start with one or two questions and build over several sessions. Here are sample questions to ask during a one-on-one How We Work conversation:

1-ON-1'S
15 QUESTIONS TO ASK TO BUILD A STRONG RELATIONSHIP

How are you **feeling** these days?

Since we last met, what are you most **proud** of and why?

What is one thing **holding you back** from getting closer to achieving your goals?

What part of your job and role **energizes** you the most and **motivates** you?

Are you getting enough **feedback**? How **frequently** do you like receiving feedback?

Are there any non-work related matters that are making it **hard** for you to **concentrate** at work?

On a scale of 1-10, how **happy** are you with your current job, duties, and position? What is **one small move** you could make to move it +1?

Do you feel your current responsibilities and job align with **your future goals?**

What is one thing you need **more of** from me? What is one thing you need **less of** from me?

What **support** do you need from me this week?

What's your **top priority** for next week?

What **accomplishments** in your career are you looking forward to this year?

What are you **committing** to between now and the next time we meet? Is there anything we **missed** that you'd like to **talk** about?

How is everything going with the people you work with/on your team? Any **interactions** you'd like to **discuss**?

Do you feel like something or someone in the company is **hindering your work** in any way?

Nicole Bianchi
WWW.NICOLEMBIANCHI.COM

If you are having the conversation with your team, the first step is everyone writes—it is a rule. Each person writes down their answers so you capture all voices in the room. Here are sample questions to ask during a team How We Work conversation:

HOW WE WORK
11 QUESTIONS TO ASK TO INTENTIONALLY SET AGREEMENTS

What's most important to you in **building relationships**?

What do **you need from me** to be successful? Here's what **I need from you**....

How should **we connect** or **communicate** outside of 1:1's? What should we expect from each other?

When is **your energy at its best** for deep work or strategic thinking?

What does an **ideal day** at work look like for you?

How can we give each other **feedback** and continuously **build** a stronger relationship together?

How can we let each other know **"we have each other's backs"**?

More of/Less of? Continue/Consider?

How do you prefer to be **challenged** or **given feedback**?

If **you** are seeing something I may not be seeing, **what's the best way to share it**?

What is the best way to **recognize** the important work **you** are doing?

If we aren't feeling aligned on a **goal, topic or priority,** what is the best way to explore what's happening?

Nicole **Bianchi**
WWW.NICOLEMBIANCHI.COM

When a new leader joins an organization, there is a sense of urgency to discover information about them—leadership style, hot buttons, and values. Quickly developing a relationship with the team using a leadership assimilation process is an ideal way to set expectations and build a strong team.

Similar to the team How We Work conversation, employees anonymously write down questions about the new leader's personal style, decision-making style, preferred communication, performance expectations, and priorities. The leader's answers often stimulate further areas of discussion for follow-up conversations and serve as building blocks for the agreements the team creates in the next steps. The following are common Leadership Assimilation Questions:

Leadership Style

- How can we tell when something is important to you?
- How do you handle disagreements/conflict?
- What are your strengths? What are the areas you continue to develop?

Communication & Problem Solving

- How should status information be presented?

- What are your preferences relative to email, phone calls, and face-to-face communication? How often?
- What are the ground rules for calling you outside of business hours?

Decision-making Style

- How far down do you intend to push the decision-making process?
- Is there a negotiation period after you make a decision—when is it over?
- How should we approach you if we have questions/concerns about a decision?

Performance Expectations

- What behaviors do you expect of us?
- What is your definition of a top performer?
- When and how will I receive performance feedback?

Your Priorities

- What is your primary business priority in the next six months?
- What are your long-term goals?
- What are your personal career goals?

Step 2: Gather input. Record answers on a large sheet of paper or whiteboard. Ask the team, "What's needed for our team to be high-performing?"

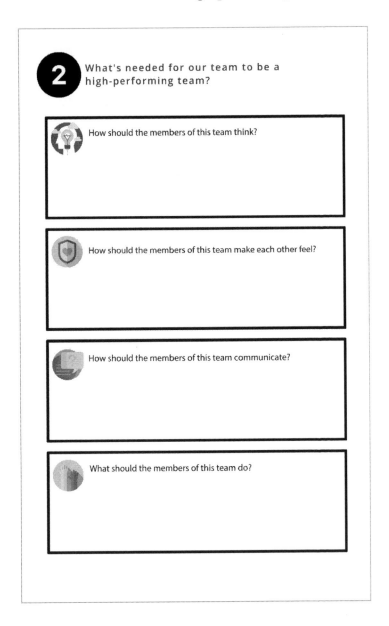

2 What's needed for our team to be a high-performing team?

How should the members of this team think?

How should the members of this team make each other feel?

How should the members of this team communicate?

What should the members of this team do?

Step 3: Create rules. Create five agreements that will serve as your rules. For one-on-one relationships, each agreement should be an idea that helps the two people have a high-performing relationship.

For a team, each agreement should be an attitude or behavior that serves the team.

3 Create a 1st draft set of agreements

Agreement #1
How will this attitude or behavior serve this team?

Agreement #2
How will this attitude or behavior serve this team?

Agreement #3
How will this attitude or behavior serve this team?

Agreement #4
How will this attitude or behavior serve this team?

Agreement #5
How will this attitude or behavior serve this team?

Step 4: Label rules. Give each agreement a title that reminds each person of the idea, behavior, or attitude. Keep it short and easy to remember. Then write a brief description—what the agreement is designed to encourage or guard against.

For example, the "Straight Talk" rule I mentioned earlier in this chapter is the title that reminds my team to be honest and up front about an issue to guard against hurt feelings and resentment.

4 **Craft your final agreements.**
Title: Give it a snappy name
Description: A brief paragraph of the behaviors + attitudes this agreement is designed to encourage or guard against.

Title #1
Description

Title #2
Description

Title #3
Description

Title #4
Description

Title #5
Description

Building Habits

Once the agreements are in place, it is time to practice the routines, or habits, that support them. One team I worked with created an agreement titled "Connect Interpersonally." They developed a routine to gather for coffee once a week in a shared space at work just to connect and talk about life.

Another team created an agreement titled "Have Friends in Technical Places." Each team member identified subject matter experts they could turn to for answers when needed. The following steps should be followed during the Building Habits portion of the How We Work conversation:

Step 1: Live the rules. Creating routines is just as important as creating the rules. The work doesn't stop with developing the agreements; it's living them so you can have strong relationships and high performance. Ownership of the rules and routines must be shared, so you need to weave the agreements into every one-on-one and team meeting. It doesn't do any good to create the rules and routines if nobody is living them.

Step 2: Review the rules. The frequency of these conversations—the rhythms—will help keep everyone aligned and provide opportunity to modify the rules if needed. Be aware of how often you and your team need to meet.

With one-on-one relationships, you might need to meet weekly at first. For a team, you should acknowledge your agreements once a month. Maybe you only need to meet for 20 or 30 minutes instead of 60 minutes.

You should also re-evaluate the agreements quarterly. Is there an agreement you should be doing more or less of? Is there an agreement that should be changed? Is there one that needs to be more specific? Don't hesitate to adjust agreements. Forming new habits takes time, and you want to ensure everyone remains in sync.

You can also have conversations at creative locations. A leader's office can be intimidating and portray a feeling of power imbalance. Consider a walking one-on-one meeting or a way to meet with a remote worker other than a video call.

Ideally, a team meets outside of the office for the initial intention setting session. When working with a team, I like to have them participate in an experience after setting the agreements—it's like icing on the cake and a way for everyone to practice being aligned.

I facilitated a How We Work session that ended with the team participating in a bike building experience.

Small groups were tasked with assembling a bicycle that was donated to a non-profit when finished.

The groups had to develop a routine for building the bikes using the rules they created during the session. Not only did they have to work together and assign tasks, but if someone made a mistake, such as attaching the handlebars backwards, team members had to trust one another to speak up and point out mistakes or offer help when needed.

Exceptional Results

It's time for you to lead a brave conversation. Think of someone you need to have the How We Work conversation with—an employee, your team, or a spouse. You can start small and create one or two agreements together and then put those agreements into action before adding another rule.

Honor your promise to adhere to the agreement and decide how often you will review it. Once you've had the conversation, return to this section and answer the following:

1. Did you establish rules, routines, and rhythms?
2. What worked well?

3. What is one thing you can improve next time?
4. Are you ready for more? Scan the QR code at the bottom of this page.

3

THE ASK

I HAD BEEN the director of HR for a company for eight years and was in the process of hiring peers from other companies within the industry. Because their salary information was visible, I realized my salary lagged significantly compared to the market—I had been working for the company since my start as an intern.

Despite the discrepancy, my performance reviews were consistently "above or exceeds expectations." I decided to ask the vice president (VP) to re-evaluate my compensation. I was incredibly nervous to have that meeting—nauseous, lightheaded, and anything but brave.

I prepared for the meeting by gathering data, which included my performance review, compensation, and information on current compensation in the market (I was at 20% of the market average whereas most people in a similar position were at 50%, so the gap had grown to between $30,000-$50,000).

During the meeting, I presented the information and asked him to review it—I sat in nervous silence, waiting for his response. He said he hadn't seen what I was seeing because he was leading a large team and it wasn't on his radar, so he thanked me for bringing it to his attention. He agreed to work with the compensation team on a review.

Two weeks later he proposed an aggressive stair-step approach to increase my compensation over the next year until I reached market level. My ask was a win. He appreciated me sharing something he wasn't seeing, and I appreciated him recognizing my value and performance at the company.

Tough Talk: The Ask

Asking for help seems so simple, but it's one of the toughest conversations for leaders to have. In a study conducted by OnePoll, only 1 in 4 Americans are willing to ask for help before starting something new.

Half of those surveyed said they wait to ask for help until the situation becomes too overwhelming, and 53% feel held back from achieving certain life goals because they try to do it alone. Jessica Jones, Senior Vice President, People & Culture with Pathward shares:

> **"Simple and hard are different—don't confuse the two. Avoiding a simple conversation because it could be hard is less efficient, doesn't make it any easier, and is less likely to create success."**

During The Ask conversation, you ask for help, permission, or acknowledgment.

Asking for Help: This is often the toughest ask because you must admit you need help with something and then decide who you are going to ask to help you. It can be especially difficult for leaders to ask their team for help because leaders feel they should have all the answers or be experienced enough to do it on their own.

I recently spoke at a conference and received a thank you email from an attendee. She shared some personal life struggles that had held her back from pursuing her dream of becoming a facilitator. At the end of my presentation, I instruct everyone to say one small act of bravery they can make. She shared:

"...When you asked us to say our small act of bravery at the end of your session, I knew I needed to just ask if you would be willing to continue the conversation and let me pick your brain. So, would you be willing to meet with me for coffee and a chance to learn from you?"

Asking for Permission: This type of ask is tough because it feels like you have a lack of control. But asking for permission is not a request from an authority figure, it is a show of respect for a relationship.

I coached a manager who had an upcoming work trip for a start-up company experiencing double-digit growth. He was struggling with several personal issues at home and felt the trip needed to be postponed.

He was afraid if he didn't go on the trip, it would have negative ramifications for his career. For three days he avoided talking to his boss because he didn't want to let his boss down by not going on the trip.

Finally, he had The Ask talk. He explained the situation at home and asked his boss for permission to postpone the trip. His boss agreed without hesitation and encouraged him to tend to his personal needs. Asking his boss for permission showed his respect, and in turn, his boss extended the same respect to him.

Travel influencer Kacie Rose shares one of the toughest conversations she's had:

> "I was in my mid 20s at a breaking point as a professional dancer in New York City —the industry can be brutal—when I found a $200 ticket to fly to Venice, Italy, while drinking a bottle of wine. I wasn't happy, so I booked my ticket at that moment.
>
> "Then I realized I had to tell my dad I was going on a solo trip. I am my dad's only child. He is a kind and warm human, but he reaction was, 'You can't do it.' He was concerned about my well being. I told him, 'I am going. I understand you are nervous and scared. I am not a child anymore. I can take care of myself.' We began to make agreements, such as I would call every day, and our conversation shifted."

Asking for Acknowledgment: With this type of ask, you seek to understand. It can feel like you are trying to persuade the other person to agree with your perspective, but acknowledgement can come without agreement.

I coached a new leader at a university, and her boss sent budgets to university department deans without sharing them with her. When a dean had a question, my client couldn't answer because she didn't have the information. I coached her on asking her boss for acknowledgement that she was being kept out of the loop.

During the conversation, her boss explained she thought she was helping by not overwhelming my client with information and meetings. As soon as she realized it was causing more problems, she changed her behavior and included my client when communicating with departments.

If my client and her boss had the How We Work conversation when my client was hired, they could have avoided The Ask conversation.

Position the Ask: Be BRAVE

When having The Ask conversation, position your ask to maximize the possibility of acceptance. The following are five steps to be BRAVE during the ask:

Step 1: **B—Background information**. It is helpful to give the other person context surrounding the situation that has led you to The Ask conversation. Provide two or three key points. Keep them brief to set the stage, and don't draw them out into a monologue.

Step 2: **R—Research-based case**. Bring facts and data to the conversation that support your ask. If it is in writing, that is even better. Provide any information that will help get you closer to yes.

Step 3: **A—Advocate and make the ask**. This tough talk is made easier by having confidence, being assertive, and staying positive. A hopeful mindset embraces the possibility of change, which is the goal of The Ask conversation.

If you come from a positive position, the other person is more open to saying yes. When you make the ask, it should be one sentence, 5-7 words total. Here are sample questions for making the ask:

THE ASK

11 QUESTIONS TO START THE CONVERSATION

I have a difficult
"ask"
I need to make...

Our relationship is
important to me,
I need to make an
ask of you...

To make sure we stay
aligned,
I would like to ask for
our **next steps**.

I want to bring
awareness to a
situation you may not
see and ask for your
perspective.

Asking for help is
challenging for me,
I would like to share
more about the
challenges in my role.

I am struggling with a
challenge
and would like to ask
you for some
feedback.

Could I **ask your
advice**
on a tough situation
I am dealing with?

I would be grateful if
you could
help me
with something...

Would you **be
willing** to
help me?

Thank you for taking the
time to meet with me,

Could I share a situation
in which I could use your
**help/assistance/
perspective**
on?

I wanted **to ask**
you something
that is
important to me...

Nicole **Bianchi**
WWW.NICOLEMBIANCHI.COM

Step 4: **V—Voice is quiet, trust the silence**.
Too many people make the ask and then keep talking.
They hem, haw, dilute the ask, or change it. Even

worse, they apologize. Never diminish your ask. Once you've made it, quiet your voice and keep silent while you wait for a response.

Step 5: **E—End with action**. Don't leave the conversation without aligning on next steps even if it is to continue the conversation later, and agree on when that will be. The action might be to monitor a situation or follow up on a behavior. If you agree to revisit the conversation, put it on the calendar.

Each person should own a piece of the action. The clearer both people are on their next steps, the higher the likelihood they will follow through. If one person doesn't hold up their end of the agreement, check in with them and ask to have another conversation.

Using these five **BRAVE** steps to position the ask will give you more confidence and a higher rate of success with this tough talk.

Brave Conversation: Asking for Help

When I started my consulting business, I wanted to gain experience by completing a few smaller projects. I reached out to four people within my professional network to ask for help.

Step 1: **B—Background information.** I let all four people know that after years of talking about starting my own business, I was finally doing it.

Step 2: **R—Research-based case.** I explained that my plan was to gain experience by consulting on smaller, individual projects.

Step 3: **A—Advocate and make the ask.** I asked each of them if they needed help on any projects.

Step 4: **V—Voice is quiet, trust the silence.** It was a difficult ask because I didn't know if they would want me to work for free, or if they were willing to work with an experienced professional yet inexperienced consultant. I made the ask and waited.

Step 5: **E—End with action.** Two of the people responded right away. Both had an immediate need for project help and provided me with their budgets and timelines. One opportunity for a Fortune 10 company helped launched my business in a powerful way.

Brave Conversation: Asking for Permission

Every year I facilitate and present at two different day-long conferences, which I have done for the past eight years. Last year, both conferences were scheduled during my 6-week trip to Italy.

My choices were to fly back in the middle of my trip and keep the obligations or ask them for permission to send someone in my place.

I was afraid they would either insist on option one or agree to option two but not book me again next year. It was a risky ask that could result in current and future lost revenue.

Step 1: **B—Background information.** I explained to each meeting planner that my husband had just retired and was taking a year off, it was our 25-year wedding anniversary, and I was using the time on vacation to write my book. It was a once in a lifetime opportunity.

Step 2: **R—Research-based case.** I also shared that I spoke with my business partner, and he agreed to facilitate both conferences. The materials and rate would be the same, and he was equally skilled.

Step 3: **A—Advocate and make the ask.** I emphasized that I wanted them to feel comfortable with the approach for this year's conference and asked them to accept a different solution than what they had been used to the past eight years.

Step 4: **V—Voice is quiet, trust the silence.** I made the asks during video meetings, so after the ask was made, I sat and waited for their response without making additional comments.

Step 5: **E—End with action.** Each of the meeting planners agreed to my ask and their reactions were kind and generous. They were genuinely excited for me and the opportunity to take the trip.

I guaranteed a seamless transition for the conferences, and they were both pleased with the results. They both also rebooked me for the following year.

Brave Conversation: Asking for acknowledgment

Have you ever worked with someone who should have shared something with you and instead shared it with others? When I was a VP of HR, I learned that the VP of sales was questioning the performance of one of my team members because they weren't working the same number of hours as the rest of the team. The information got back to me, so I requested a meeting with the VP of sales.

Step 1: **B—Background information.** I informed him that I had been receiving feedback from other employees about his concerns regarding the performance of my team member.

Step 2: **R—Research-based case.** I explained that her role and responsibilities didn't require her to work the same number of hours as the rest of the team.

Step 3: **A—Advocate and make the ask.** I asked that going forward, concerns about my team members be brought to me directly before discussing it with anyone else.

Step 4: **V—Voice is quiet, trust the silence.** He acknowledged having the concerns and that he'd been discussing it with other employees.

Step 5: **E—End with action.** He agreed that going forward, he would come to me first with any concerns. He smiled, shook my hand, and thanked me for having the conversation.

Asking for acknowledgement can prevent relationships from deteriorating and help you avoid tougher conversations later.

The Ask conversation requires bravery because it feels so personal. If you detach from that feeling and keep the ask clear and concise, it leads to a better result and gives you more confidence for next time. It's easy to assume the other person sees what you see—that's a mistake.

Instead, assuming positive intention and making the ask will bring the attention needed. It also helps to be open to options—not everyone will agree to your ask. Ending with an action to simply continue the conversation is a great way to maintain a positive relationship with the person.

Exceptional Results

It's time for you to lead a brave conversation. Think of someone you need to have The Ask conversation with —an employee, a spouse, or a friend. Maybe you ask your spouse to help you plan the next family vacation and divide tasks so you are both accountable for the trip going smoothly. Or a coworker repeatedly interrupts you throughout the day and you ask them to acknowledge the behavior. Once you've had the conversation, return to this section and answer the following:

1. Did you follow the **BRAVE** steps for the ask?
2. What worked well?
3. What is one thing you can improve next time?
4. Are you ready for more? Scan the QR code at the bottom of this page.

WHAT'S GOING ON?

SEVERAL YEARS AGO, GE Aviation hired me to facilitate a meeting with British Airways at GE's Crotonville Leadership Institute in New York, which is a sprawling campus filled with cutting edge leadership programming and experiences.

The two companies had been partners for decades and hired me because negotiations had stalled between the two companies for almost 12 months.

It was important to the GE Aviation sales team to restart negotiations to sell the engines to British Airways. The stakes were high. GE Aviation thought if they gifted British Airways some expertise and best practices it would aid in resuming negotiations.

I was initially hired to showcase and share best practices we had implemented in Teaming, Coaching, and

Leadership Development at the 80+ GE Aviation sites with British Airways—essentially a dog and pony show. It was obvious British Airways wasn't interested in dogs or ponies.

I'm an intuitive person, and during the first session, I sensed that something wasn't quite right—the British Airways attendees weren't making eye contact with me, they were checking their phones, and leaders from each company were sitting on opposite sides of the room.

During the first break, I spoke to several attendees from each company. The GE leaders, who had been with the company for only a few months, assured me that everything was going great, but the British Airways leaders, who had been with the company for many years, said there was some history between the two companies that wasn't being acknowledged. They appreciated my coaching but wanted to have some deeper conversations with GE.

After the break, I pivoted my presentation and focused on asking the attendees to help me create a timeline of the relationship between the two companies: where it started, where it was now, and the direction it needed to go.

During this discussion, GE's VP of sales left the room. After about 15 minutes, the leaders from British

Airways began asking about him. I told everyone to take a break and found the GE leader outside on his phone.

I waited for him to finish his call and asked, "What's going on? Why did you leave the meeting?" He assured me everything was fine, and said, "You got this."

I explained that we were discussing some critical information about the relationship between the two companies, and he needed to be in the room.

We returned and learned the British Airways leaders had been there for the past 15 years, whereas GE rotated leaders every 18-24 months. Eight years prior, there had been a big misunderstanding between the two companies—the leaders from British Airways hadn't forgotten, and the current GE leaders had no knowledge of it.

The rest of the conversation focused on what British Airways leaders needed to alleviate their fears and how the two companies could move forward with their relationship and mutual commitments. We finished the meeting strong and aligned on how the two teams were going to move forward. We celebrated the fact negotiations would resume by holding a culinary team-building experience.

Tough Talk: What's Going On?

The What's Going On? conversation explores a shift in someone's behavior, performance, or relationship. At first glance, having this talk might not seem that difficult, but there are several factors that can make it messy. First, the conversation addresses a problem, so it is fueled by emotion.

Second, most people don't know how to start the conversation, so they default to using the wrong tactics. This blocks the path to having a meaningful conversation. To identify when to have the What's Going On? conversation, you need to understand the types of changes someone can exhibit.

Behavior: A shift in a person's behavior is usually something small and starts suddenly—they show up late to a few meetings, they aren't as responsive to emails, or they seem quieter at work. It is easy to observe but also easy to ignore.

Performance: A shift in a person's performance that points to a trend in the wrong direction, such as missing deadlines or a slight decline in work quality.

Relationship: A shift in a person's relationship can manifest in how they interact with you or how they interact with the team. An example is an employee who doesn't speak up during a meeting but has side conversations about the meeting with co-workers afterward. If you've had the How We Work conversation and established the rules, routines, and rhythms, a shift in relationship should be easy to spot.

In all three situations, if a leader ignores the shift, then the individual will continue down the negative path and assume the leader has noticed but doesn't care enough to say anything. At that point, it will quickly escalate into a Being Better or Moving On conversation.

Unlike conversations for How We Work and The Ask, the goal of What's Going On? is to achieve resolution. This requires three coaching moves:

Step 1: **Build understanding.** Share your observations about the shift in behavior, performance, or relationship to bring awareness to the situation. This is where the conversation can stall before getting off the ground.

When a leader doesn't know how to start, they default to side-stepping the issue and asking, "I just want to check in—how are you?" The person will always respond, "I'm fine." The leader may also point out the shift in situation and ask, "What's wrong?" The person will take a defensive stance and answer, "Nothing." It is imperative as a leader to approach the conversation with a neutral, objective mindset, ask better questions, and listen to understand. Below is a list of What's Going On? conversation starters:

WHAT'S GOING ON

11 QUESTIONS TO START THE CONVERSATION

You don't have to go at this **alone**, I am here, what would be **helpful** to talk about?

I want to **check-in** and see how you are doing. What is a **challenge** you are facing right now?

I have noticed you have been **frustrated** lately; what can I do to help you?

I've noticed your **energy** shifted when we started talking about xxx, what's up?

I've **noticed** you have been really quiet this past week; I wanted to **check-in** to see how you are doing?

I **appreciate** your positive energy over the past few weeks; it shows! What is **re-enenergizing** you right now?

Here is how I am seeing the current situation, I want to **explore** what might be going on...

What is one thing that is **going well** for you right now?

We had **aligned** on the next steps, yet I do not see any **action** from you.

What's going on?

What is one thing you are focused on **improving**?

Our **relationship** is **important** to me, and I feel like we haven't been on the **same page** recently.

You seem **agitated** when I bring up **challenges**, talk to me about what's going on?

What is **one thing** we could change for the better?

Nicole **Bianchi**
WWW.NICOLEMBIANCHI.COM

How you start this talk will set the tone for the rest of the conversation. There has a to be a genuine, caring aspect to your inquiry that ends with, "I'd like to talk about what's going on." Denice Biocca, Chief Human Resources Officer for GE Gas and Power shares:

> **"State your intentions up front: 'I really want you to grow, and there is something in the way.' 'I value our relationship and would like to see it get stronger.' 'We need your brain power on our team.' 'There is space to fail here. I want to make sure we are learning from our setbacks and mistakes.'"**

Step 2: **Build alignment.** Both parties acknowledge the situation, listen to each other, and mutually explore individual desired outcomes and whether those outcomes align.

Step 3: **Build action.** This establishes the next move and where to go from here. When it is a behavior or performance situation, the leader should not source the change.

You can edit and enhance it, but the individual should suggest the solution so they don't overpromise and underdeliver. If it is a relationship situation, you may have to revisit the How We Work rules and routines to realign.

Brave Conversation: Shift in Behavior

During my corporate career, I was in a CHRO role in charge of hiring an HR manager for our Henderson, NV, office, located on the outskirts of Las Vegas. The existing staff in that office were inexperienced and exhibiting unacceptable behavior—"what happens in Vegas stays in Vegas" type of activities—so I needed someone onsite who could manage them.

I had narrowed it down to a final candidate who had been exemplary in every interview, so I invited the director of operations to interview her. He flew into town, and we scheduled a dinner interview. The candidate arrived on time, sat down at the table, we chatted, and ordered food. A few minutes later she excused herself to go to the ladies' room.

Five minutes passed, then 10 minutes, and then 15 minutes. I didn't want to be rude in case she needed more time, but I decided to check on her. She was not in the restroom nor outside the front door of the restaurant—she had vanished.

I returned to the table, and the waiter was serving our dinner. My colleague and I were confused and assumed she had ditched the interview, so we decided to go ahead and eat. It was the first time in my 15-year HR career I had ever had this happen (then again, it was Vegas).

We had almost finished our meals when the candidate walked back to the table, sat down, and placed her toddler in the chair next to her. Without any explanation, she picked up where the conversation had left off.

I ordered food for her child, and we continued the interview, assuming she would explain what happened. Instead, she continued as if nothing had happened.

The next day, she called me and expressed how excited she was about the job opportunity. I couldn't avoid the What's Going On? conversation.

Step 1: **Build understanding.** I politely addressed the fact that she left in the middle of the job interview without explanation and that we felt abandoned. Further, she returned with her child without saying a word. I wanted to understand and asked her what was going on.

Step 2: **Build alignment.** She explained she received a text that her daycare arrangements during the interview had fallen through and she needed to immediately pick up her child. She apologized—she didn't know she would be gone that long.

Step 3: **Build action.** I emphasized it would have been better for her to be honest with us. Because she couldn't trust us with that information, I didn't feel I could trust her with managing the office, so unfortunately there was no way to move forward.

Brave Conversation: Shift in Performance

At another Fortune 300 company I was the senior director of HR, and my executive vice president (EVP) hired a friend to conduct executive coaching sessions. The coach had an impressive resume and charged the company a hefty weekly rate, so expectations were high. My role was to determine which leaders participated in coaching, schedule the sessions, and manage the coach.

Four months into the arrangement, a few of the leaders approached me individually. Some felt they were no longer benefitting from the sessions, and others requested to stop them altogether. I asked questions to get additional information, and finally one of them was brave enough to share the truth.

That week the coach wore the same pair of pants each day, and it had a hole near the crotch. During the sessions, he fidgeted with the hole, placing his finger inside it. I confirmed this with other leaders and brought it to my EVP's attention. We aligned on the next step—I needed to have the What's Going On? talk with the coach.

Step 1: **Build understanding.** I opened the conversation by acknowledging that what he was about to hear was going to be uncomfortable. Without judgement, I explained that several leaders he had met with that week had observed that the pants he wore every day had a hole near the crotch, which he fidgeted with and poked his finger in and out of during the sessions. I pointed out that he was wearing the pants again that day and asked him What's Going On?

Step 2: **Build alignment.** He made excuses and insisted that leaders had misread the situation. I could have accepted his weak answers, but I knew I needed to build alignment, so I kept asking questions until he admitted that he had recently encountered struggles in his personal life and wasn't coping with them well. I had to lean in.

Step 3: **Build action.** I told him the only acceptable solution was to leave the office and come back with a new pair of pants. If he didn't have a different pair at his hotel, I offered to call a taxi and provided suggestions for clothing stores. He agreed, left, and came back later that day, wearing a new pair of pants. It was a small action that resolved a large issue.

Brave Conversation: Shift in Relationship

I was in an HR leadership position and transitioning from supporting one area of the business to another. I had a good working relationship with the woman taking over my previous role.

A month into my new position, colleagues shared that she was making negative comments about how I left unfinished projects for her to clean up. After hearing several accounts, I knew it was time to have the What's Going On? talk with her.

Step 1: **Build understanding.** I asked her to meet for coffee and shared the comments that colleagues told me she had made. I then paused and asked, "What's going on?" trusting silence and waiting for her to respond.

Step 2: **Build alignment.** She immediately began to cry and explained that she felt overwhelmed and intimidated—she didn't feel she could "fill my shoes" because of the strong relationships I had and the results we had achieved together, so she made disparaging comments about me to prove her own worth. I was surprised and had no idea she felt this way.

Step 3: **Build action.** I assured her I wanted her to be successful in the role and that I wanted to help her any way I could. We made a plan for how I could better help her with the transition. People often make assumptions, but when you take time to ask what's going on, you get to the heart of the issue and are able to realign.

The What's Going On? talk should be one that you are having as often as needed no matter how uncomfortable it might be. If I can tell my EVP's friend to stop playing with the hole in the crotch of his pants, you can have awkward, tough What's Going On? conversations too.

The more you practice them, the easier they get, resulting in exceptional leadership that is admired and respected. The What's Going On? conversation is tougher than the previous two because it highlights a negative issue that is causing tension.

It is uncomfortable and often emotional for both parties, but when you don't have the conversation, it accelerates to a Being Better conversation.

Although most leaders acknowledge it is awkward, they are relieved and pleased after having the What's Going On? conversation. The following illustrates that range of emotion:

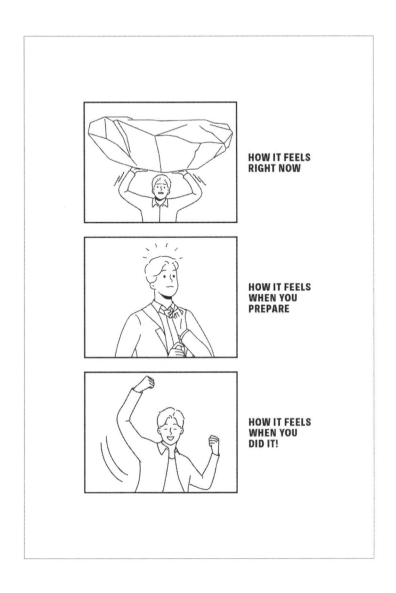

HOW IT FEELS
RIGHT NOW

HOW IT FEELS
WHEN YOU
PREPARE

HOW IT FEELS
WHEN YOU
DID IT!

Exceptional Results

Have you noticed a shift in someone's behavior, performance, or their relationship with you? If so, it's time to lead a brave What's Going On? conversation with them. Choose one of the conversation starters from the beginning of this chapter. Once you've had the conversation, return to this section and answer the following:

1. How did you start the conversation?
2. Did you follow all three steps and end with action?
3. What worked well?
4. What is one thing you can improve next time?
5. Are you ready for more? Scan the QR code at the bottom of this page.

BEING BETTER

DURING MY TIME AS A CHRO, the company I worked for was sold, and my role was to determine which systems, processes, and benefits the new company would keep. The position required me to travel to Richmond, VA, every other week to meet with the acquisition team.

Because their systems were antiquated, I was tasked with persuading them to adopt our systems, which wasn't easy. Every Monday I flew out with energy and excitement only to return home every Friday, feeling frustrated and defeated that I wasn't making progress.

After about six months, my husband sat me down to have a conversation. From a place of love and concern, he told me that I had become miserable to be around and that I needed to be better at home for him and for our young kids. The words hit me like a wave, and I knew he was right. I felt like I wasn't being successful at work or at home, and I knew the situation wasn't going to get better.

I suggested looking for a different HR role, but my husband asked, "What about starting the consulting business you've been talking about?"

I told him I didn't have it planned yet, and he asked me, "What's the worst that could happen?" I answered that it could fail. He then asked, "If it fails, can you still find an HR job?" I realized that I could, which was a huge relief.

My next move was to slowly build my leadership development and coaching business, and six months later I was fully launched. I never had to get another HR job, and I've had my business for 10 years.

When someone isn't at their best, rather than simply pointing out what they are doing wrong, you can have a conversation to help them define what being better looks like. An exceptional leader holds a mirror in front of the person so they can explore a solution.

Tough Talk: Being Better

The Being Better talk confronts an issue related to someone's behavior or performance. Whereas the

What's Going On? conversation focuses on a sudden change, the Being Better conversation connects the dots to reveal a pattern over time.

This talk requires bravery because you must point out someone's shortcomings. But doing so out of a place of care and concern will help improve your relationships. Heather Ray, CEO of Christian Nobel Furs shares:

> **"I hate confrontation and having tough conversations, but you have to put feelings —yours and theirs—aside to help someone grow or to change a situation. If they are willing to learn, grow, or change, they will be thankful for you taking the time to teach them."**

There are two types of Being Better conversations:

Behavior: Confronting an issue related to how someone is behaving. This behavior could be with their mood, attitude, or approach toward people and situations. They may share their own versions of the truth, make passive aggressive comments, or undermine their leaders.

Performance: Confronting an issue related to someone's performance. This could include missing multiple deadlines on a project, not meeting daily or weekly goals, or not doing their part on a team project.

When an issue with behavior or performance becomes a pattern, don't ignore it. The person may not even realize it's an issue. If they are fully aware and you don't say anything, then they may assume you don't care. Either way, the issue can quickly escalate and turn into a Moving On conversation.

There are five steps to follow when having a Being Better conversation (adapted from the Center for Creative Leadership):

Step 1: **Situation.** Describe the behavior or performance issue that has become a pattern. Be specific and stick to the facts. If you want to first test the waters, you can start by asking, "What are three things you feel you are doing well? What are two ways you are actively improving?" You can also start the conversation with one of these examples:

BEING BETTER

11 CONVERSATION STARTERS

I want to **share** something with you that may be **uncomfortable to hear**...

Here's how you can **win**, here is how you can **fail**...

You **aren't at your best** right now.
I need to **share a pattern** I am beginning to see emerge....

My **intent** is to be candid with you and **share** what I am **observing**...

I **care** about you.
I need ___ to **change** for you to be **successful**.

Things aren't going well right now for you.
We need to **discuss** how to get it back on track.

Here is how I **see** the **facts** and the situation...

The **feedback** I am about to share isn't good.
You have a **choice**.
You can shrink or
You can **do something** about it.

I am going to **share** something with you that may be **difficult** for you to **hear**.

I need to **share** something with you that is **uncomfortable** for **me** and could be **uncomfortable** for **you**.

I **care** about **you**.
I care about your **success**.

I need to share **concerns** I have regarding your performance.

*Nicole*Bianchi
WWW.NICOLEMBIANCHI.COM

Step 2: **Observation.** Describe the observable behavior without judgement. Avoid assuming you know what the other person is thinking or how they will react.

Step 3: **Impact.** Explain the impact their behavior or performance has had on other people and the company. Be clear about the impact—have people lost trust? Have the company's results been affected?

Step 4: **Explore.** Give the person a chance to respond and share their story. Allow them to have accountability.

Step 5: **Action.** Let the person take the lead on crafting next steps to get out of the situation and what needs to happen so they can improve and become better.

Brave Conversation: Issue with Behavior

I was hired to coach an onsite quality assurance (QA) leader for a manufacturing facility. My role included meeting with stakeholders, gathering initial feedback, implementing changes, and then gathering subsequent feedback and reporting results.

Our first sessions were to develop a relationship and gather information. Next, I moved into the phase where I gathered feedback from stakeholders. Going in, I knew the stakeholders had issues with the QA leader's behavior, but it was far worse than I had imagined. On a scale of 1-5, with 5 being a great leader, she had scores as low as 0.

I learned that when she started her position, the plant was in remediation, which meant legally it couldn't operate. They needed a leader who was assertive and could issue directives to get the plant up and running quickly.

My client had successfully pulled them out of remediation and continued to lead in the same manner. Unfortunately, her forceful, assertive approach did not promote collaboration with her team going forward, but nobody had pointed this out to her. It was now my job to lead a Being Better talk with her.

Step 1: **Situation.** I started the conversation by letting her know that I needed to share feedback that may be uncomfortable, but as her coach, I would be there to support and work together with her.

Step 2: **Observation.** I explained that the feedback I had gathered wasn't good, and shared the negative feedback in a very factual manner.

Step 3: **Impact.** Her behavior and leadership style had damaged relationships with her team, and they didn't feel they could trust her.

Step 4: **Explore.** She cried when she heard the feedback but quickly realized her mistakes. She wanted to work on a path forward and repair the relationships. Her goal was to work with people who would help lift her up.

Step 5: **Action.** I wanted her to rise to the occasion rather than shrink and retreat, so I coached her on having individual conversations with each of her team members. We crafted the messages so she could be authentic, vulnerable, and admit her shortcomings.

The person who originally rated her a zero wasn't aware of the challenges she faced when she first arrived at the plant. She worked hard at being better and went on to have a successful career there.

Leaders often move through their careers without having anyone help them see what they aren't seeing. When this happens, it quickly escalates into a Being Better conversation.

Brave Conversation: Issue with Performance

One of my team members had been promoted to the compensation and benefits manager. Based on her past experience, I thought she would be able to expertly manage the role.

About six months in, I received feedback from different benefits vendors that she had missed several deadlines and wasn't allowing adequate time to review data. We had already communicated information to employees, and the promised dates for them to receive compensation in their paycheck was in jeopardy. I requested a meeting in her office to lead a Being Better conversation.

Step 1: **Situation.** I started the conversation by letting her know that I cared about her and her success and needed to share concerns regarding her performance.

Step 2: **Observation.** It was clear she had missed several important deadlines because she wasn't organized and putting in the necessary time—sticky notes covered her desk and computer, which pointed to her lack of organization.

Step 3: **Impact.** Because she had missed several deadlines, we were in danger of not delivering on the promises already made to employees, and we were losing trust and confidence with the senior leadership team.

Step 4: **Explore.** At first, she talked quickly and took the conversation in random directions, but finally she acknowledged that her system of using sticky notes was not organized and didn't allow her to take work home when necessary.

She also wasn't putting in the hours needed to complete the project, and when she was at the office, she wasn't efficient with her time. She also never stopped to ask for help—I was surprised she had missed deadlines but would have helped if I had known.

Step 5: **Action.** We revised the original timeline and aligned on steps to meet those new deadlines. I also asked for daily updates to keep her on task at work. We were able to complete the project by the completion date that had been promised to employees.

Brave Conversation: Initiate for Yourself

Everyone has experienced times when they aren't at their best. You may instinctively feel it but unable to pinpoint the issue. It's okay to initiate a Being Better conversation on your own behalf. When I was first hired in my CHRO role, the executive team informed me if I couldn't improve the department, they would outsource it all, so the stakes were high.

There was so much to fix, I didn't spend as much time developing relationships. Instead, I focused on addressing the issues. I realized I wasn't receiving feedback from any of the leaders and worried it was because I wasn't doing my job well. That prompted me to have a Being Better conversation with my leader.

Step 1: **Situation.** I started the conversation by asking my leader what he thought I was doing well and what he thought I could improve. He turned the question around and asked *me* to answer those questions.

Step 2: **Observation.** I told him I thought we were adding value to the company because the systems and processes were helping make everyone's job easier, but I wasn't receiving positive feedback from the leadership team.

Step 3: **Impact.** I worried that I hadn't spent enough time building relationships with the leadership team, which left them with a negative impression and distrust for what my team was doing. I needed their buy-in with the next steps and was worried I wouldn't get it.

Step 4: **Explore.** My leader explained that the previous CHRO had not performed, so they were fired. As a result, the leadership team was skeptical of my ability, and jumping into the work without spending time building relationships fed into that doubt.

Step 5: **Action.** We decided I needed to spend quality time building relationships with the leadership team and work more closely with them to identify how to address their needs. Rather than view HR as transactional, it should be a strategic partnership with each business unit.

The Being Better conversation is one of the toughest because it means someone has fallen short, and it's your job to bring it to light. But having this conversation shows you care about them and want to help improve their current situation before it becomes worse. Because it requires a level of vulnerability, it will also help improve trust, which is vital for any relationship. Master Coach Susan Mann says:

> **"Some issues won't be resolved in one conversation. It's helpful to create spaciousness and breathing room—give myself and the other person time to absorb thoughts and feelings, and time to reflect on what action to take."**

Exceptional Results

If you've noticed an issue related to someone's behavior or performance, it's time to lead a brave Being Better conversation with them. Choose one of the conversation starters from the beginning of this chapter. Once you've had the conversation, return to this section and answer the following:

1. How did you start the conversation?
2. Did you follow all five steps and end with action?
3. What worked well?
4. What is one thing you can improve next time?
5. Are you ready for more? Scan the QR code at the bottom of this page.

6

MOVING ON

WHEN I WORKED in HR at Conagra Brands, the company had its first workforce reduction. My role was to have individual conversations with the employees being laid off and present their severance packages.

My department spent the days leading up to the layoffs behind closed doors in the war room, preparing packages. The night before, it hit me how difficult the conversations were going to be—people's lives would be changed, and it made me so sad.

The next morning, I sat in my office and breathed, setting my intentions that everyone I spoke with that day would be okay. I was nervous, scared, and despised that part of my job. I didn't like the idea of forcing people to move on. The first employee entered the room, and I read through my script.

Before I had a chance to present the severance package, he stood, walked around the conference table, and hugged me. He shared that he had wanted to move on from the company to pursue other interests, but he didn't know how and was grateful the company afforded him the opportunity to do so.

In that moment, I realized I could deliver my message to individuals in an empathetic way and change the conversations to focus on a path forward rather than focus on the departure.

Tough Talk: Moving On

This talk is the toughest to have because it is always a departure from what was. Whether it's your choice to move on or someone else's, having the conversation requires a healthy dose of bravery. Annamarie Mann, Chief Enterprise Design & Transition Officer with Upstream shares:

> **"Having a tough conversation is not about being 'right.' Tough conversations are about both parties and require you to consider the relational dynamics of the**

conversation as you participate with the other person."

Moving On doesn't always mean someone is terminated from their job—it is moving on from a position, a project, or a relationship. All three types of Moving On conversations include action and a path forward. In most cases, the Moving On conversation can be avoided by successfully implementing the first four types of conversations.

Departure from position: This type of conversation is often initiated by an employee because they are dissatisfied with their leadership. According to a study conducted by Development Dimensions International, 57% of employees quit their jobs because of their boss —not their company.

My daughter, Moe, was recently in a new role and practiced the first three tough talks: How We Work, The Ask, and What's Going On. She was in a high-growth start-up company experiencing significant dysfunction with organization leaders.

After a challenging eight months, she realized nothing would change and the culture was worsening (you can only control how *you* show up). It was time for the Moving On conversation. She prepared and asked to meet face-to-face, but the CEO ducked out of their team meeting early, forcing her to have a phone conversation instead.

She scripted and prepared for the conversation and anticipated his reactions (she knew he was a deflector and challenger). During the discussion he questioned her integrity and responded with selfish statements such as, "How could you do to this me?"

Moe remained calm, removed emotion by stating only facts, and repeated her message. She made all the right moves to move on from a tough conversation.

Departure from project: As a leader, you will probably have to make the decision to move on from a project because it is in the best interest of your company.

A CEO hired me to coach his entire leadership team for a significant fee. I started by having the How We Work conversation with him to set our agreements. One of the rules was he needed to model how to successfully handle conflict. During my sessions with the leaders, they told me the CEO wasn't holding up that agreement and consciously sabotaging it.

I went back to the CEO and had The Ask conversation—I asked him to acknowledge his behavior. He admitted it but also informed me he had no intention of modeling the behaviors expected of his leadership team. In fact, he said, "I am too old. It is too late to change who I am."

I knew the coaching sessions couldn't be successful going forward, so two days later I had the Moving On conversation with him.

It was difficult giving up that much revenue, but it was in everyone's best interest, so I ended the project and refunded the unused portion of the fee.

Departure from relationship: If you have had the first four types of tough talks—particularly Being Better— and still can't align with someone, then it may be time to move on from the relationship. In these instances, the other person knows where things are headed and makes the decision to move on.

This conversation is a way for you to take control of a situation that is no longer serving the position or the project. If you neglect to have the Being Better conversation first, then it could get messy because the other person has no idea the Moving On talk is coming.

In most cases—the workforce reduction example is an exception—the Moving On conversation should never come as a surprise.

When I was hired as a CHRO, I replaced a leader the team cared about and didn't want to see move on. One of my managers struggled with the change and was reluctant to align with the new direction I set. After a year, I had a Moving On conversation with her.

I explained that I understood she was grieving the loss of the relationship with her former leader, but it wasn't serving the position or the work we were doing.

I told her she could stay in her position and be a champion for the direction we were headed, or we could discuss a transition out of her position. She decided to Move On from our relationship and transition out of her position.

There are three steps to follow during a Moving On conversation:

Step 1: **The decision.** This is the decision that has been made regarding moving on from a position, project, or relationship. Use straightforward, factual language. Here are examples of Moving On conversation starters:

Step 2: **The reason.** This is the explanation for the decision. It is important to state the decision first and the reason second to avoid confusion during the conversation. Think of the decision as the "what" and the reason as the "why." The reason should be clear and concise—clarity is kindness.

Step 3: **The action.** This communicates what is going to happen next. It could be an immediate departure, a transition, or a new way of doing things. You might also present a few options and let the person decide.

Brave Conversation: Departure from Position

Ten years into my first HR job, I was a top performer, senior leader, (I had just received a 100% bonus) and on track to be promoted to a new senior leadership position. Unfortunately, a lot of dysfunction existed at that level with other leaders, and I didn't want to be part of that environment.

I also knew if I wanted to be marketable to another company, I needed to make the move, so I made the decision to leave and already had another position secured.

My boss was one of the toxic leaders, and unfortunately, I wasn't skilled at embracing tough conversations. I never had a Being Better conversation with her or her boss. I assumed her boss knew about the dysfunctional behavior and chose not to address it.

I scheduled a meeting with my leader and her boss to have the Moving On talk. I prepared my resignation letter, practiced my script, and reminded myself to be brave.

Step 1: **The decision.** I walked into the meeting and informed my leader and her boss that I had made the decision to leave the company because I had accepted another job opportunity.

Step 2: **The reason.** Rather than address the dysfunction with my boss—I felt it wouldn't serve anyone because I had already made the decision to leave—I simply stated that I wanted other opportunities.

Step 3: **The action.** I told them I would give them four weeks so I could ensure a successful transition and help my replacement, and I handed them the envelope with my resignation letter.

Because I had not had any previous tough talks with them, they were both shocked. In fact, my boss's leader had his own envelope—a promotion offer, which I didn't open.

He was so blindsided and upset, he called the company's legal department and wanted to have me escorted out of the building that day. Thankfully, legal didn't do that. Instead, they instructed me to have another conversation with my boss's leader.

I apologized to him for not listening to his offer and explained I felt if I had read it, I would change my mind. I also articulated how difficult it was for me to make the decision to leave. He said he understood, but our relationship was already damaged. I left the company feeling like I hadn't handled it well.

Six months later, I scheduled a dinner with him because I wanted to tell him the truth about why I left the company. He agreed to meet, and I outlined the dysfunction and toxicity I had experienced.

When I left the company, I thought sharing the information would cause more problems, but I knew I should have been brave enough to have those tough talks with him. He listened, and we both left with a better understanding of the situation and re-strengthened our relationship.

Brave Conversation: Departure from Project

The head of a company's HR department asked me to coach one of their leaders who had received complaints from two female employees that the individual harassed them.

The company felt a strong female could coach the leader how to change his behavior—he was a senior VP of sales and a top producer for the company. The company had already taken away his bonus and repositioned the female employees so they were no longer his direct reports.

Step 1: **The decision.** I informed the company's HR director that I would not coach the senior VP of sales.

Step 2: **The reason.** Coaching him would be a no-win situation for everybody and send the message that the company values sales results above its people.

Step 3: **The action.** I coached the head of HR on how to persuade the CEO to have the Moving On conversation with the VP of sales. I helped him create three options that the CEO could present for what moving on might look like, the timing, and positioning it with the rest of the company.

Although I didn't accept the project, eight weeks later the HR leader called me and said the CEO successfully had the Moving On talk with the VP of sales and he no longer worked at the company. Sometimes a leader or coach's presence in a situation becomes the intervention.

Brave Conversation: Departure from Relationship

The most difficult conversation you can have is one that involves Moving On from a relationship with a loved one, especially when facing one's passing. I worked at a company with an executive leader who was diagnosed with ALS, and he knew how traumatic his journey would be. While he was able, he had a tough Moving On conversation with his family.

Step 1: **The decision.** He told them when he could no longer take care of himself, he asked that his wife and children honor his wishes to let him move on.

Step 2: **The reason.** He had done a lot of planning to ensure they would be taken care of after he was gone, and he didn't want to burden them and prolong the inevitable.

Step 3: **The action.** When the time came that he could no longer dress, bathe, and feed himself, his family didn't hesitate to selflessly honor his wishes.

One of the reasons the Moving On talk feels so scary is because people assume it is always negative, but that is not the case. Think of it as simply a departure from what was. That departure can take on many forms over varied lengths of time.

Amy Jansen-LaFontaine is my cousin and friend who was diagnosed with stage IV lung cancer that had metastasized to her brain. After battling for five years, her doctor informed her the treatments were doing more damage than good so he decided to stop them.

Suddenly, she was told, at best, she only had three months to live. Her husband was with her when she received the news, but she had to tell her parents and her children.

"My goal was to live long enough to watch my kids graduate, and I got to do that. Now we had to have a moving on conversation. I told my husband I wanted him to make sure he takes good care of the kids and he will not ever leave them. I want him to still live on my parent's land and stay close to them."

Moving on conversations can be filled with requests and intentions. She continued:

"I told my kids I really want them to make sure they all stay together and not fight— to always love each other. I told my parents to make sure my kids don't get overwhelmed and that they get my inheritance. I think the most important advice when having a tough conversation is just stay positive."

The conversation always comes from a place of genuine care and is for the benefit of everyone involved. The goal is to become so comfortable at the first three conversations, you rarely have to initiate a

Being Better or Moving On conversation. But if you do, it can be successful.

Exceptional Results

If you've reached a point with someone where you've had the first four conversations and a position, project, or relationship is no longer serving anybody, then it is time to acknowledge it and lead a brave Moving On conversation. Choose one of the conversation starters from the beginning of this chapter. Once you've had the conversation, return to this section and answer the following:

1. How did you start the conversation?
2. Did you follow all the steps and end with action?
3. What worked well?
4. What is on thing you can improve next time?
5. Are you ready for more? Scan the QR code at the bottom of this page.

7

THE TOUGH TALK PROCESS

AS AN ENTREPRENEUR, speaker, mom, and wife with a demanding schedule, I needed an activity for myself. I made a small brave move and signed up for an adult hip hop class at the dance studio where my daughter took lessons. I am clumsy and not graceful, so dance lessons would challenge me.

Every Monday evening, I joined other adults where we learned short routines and had fun together. At one of the sessions, our instructor announced that we'd be performing a choreographed routine at the upcoming studio-wide recital. There was an awkward silence similar to walking into a small town cafe and the music suddenly stops. I quickly realized that practicing one night per week was not going to be enough—I needed a process to be ready to perform.

I scheduled regular small-group practices at my house four times a week. We improved at each practice, gaining confidence along the way. I wanted to reach a point where I didn't worry about the moves and instead had fun. The night of the recital was a big success thanks to the process that allowed us to improve and build confidence.

The Process

A process doesn't need to be perfect; it needs to build habits. Improvement is impossible without a process, which forces discipline, structure, and routine. It can be refined and customized to fit your needs and goals. Every process encompasses three phases:

Before the talk: There is just as much that goes into preparing for the conversation as having the conversation itself. People often let a conversation swim in their head, and the simple act of pulling it out provides clarity.

During the talk: Managing your emotions by staying neutral and objective is critical during a tough talk. If you need to pivot, experiment by asking different questions in concise ways, and always end the conversation with alignment.

After the talk: You will only improve at having tough talks if you reflect on them and determine what went well and what you can do differently next time. Make sure you are clear on what your next move needs to be.

Creating a process for a tough talk is similar to having a process for a fitness routine. Before launching into exercise, you need to eat so you have fuel, stretch, and warm up. During your workout, you have specific moves but often experiment with other exercises or alter your routine. When you're finished, you have to take time to cool down and recover before going on to the next part of your day.

Before the Talk

At the beginning of this book, I stated that the reason people are terrible at tough talks is because they don't know how to do them. Creating a process to build routines and habits is the only way to learn how. There are four steps to follow before ever having the conversation:

Step 1: **Prep.** Take time to focus on what is in front of you. Write down your thoughts, feelings, and needs before the conversation to provide clarity and put you in the right frame of mind. Write down your answers to these seven questions:

1. What are the facts of this situation?
2. How do you feel about the situation at this moment—surprise, fear, anger, sadness, or frustration?
3. What is the desired outcome for you and for the other person?
4. What is important for you to let them know?
5. What are you most curious about?
6. What part of the situation do you own—did something slip through the cracks? Was a promise not fulfilled? Did you have competing priorities?
7. How urgent is this situation—does it need to be addressed today, tomorrow, or within the next week?

This assessment is key to driving action and accountability for the process. It helps build self-awareness so you don't second-guess your feelings about a situation or your goals for the conversation. Annamarie Mann with Upstream says:

> **"Before every tough conversation, I challenge myself to consider my intentions and the relational dynamics between me and the other party. 'What do I hope to gain or achieve by having this conversation?' Be honest! I make sure I can articu-**

late this intention before having the conversation."

Step 2: **Script.** No two tough conversations will be exactly the same, so you must draft a script to ensure you communicate your goals. Drafting a script includes the following:

1. *Conversation starter.* The first few sentences are the most important, so write those down. Depending on which type of talk you are leading, choose one of the conversation starters suggested in each chapter. Do not water down your language or apologize for the conversation.

2. *Share the situation.* Write down two or three perspectives of the situation as you see them.

3. *Explore.* Ask powerful questions to go deeper into the situation and understand the other person's thoughts and feelings.

4. *Align.* Finish your script with one or two questions that achieve alignment and action. The questions should intentionally direct the other person to assume ownership of the action. Below are sample questions to close and gain alignment:

- Let's discuss and align on our (or your) next steps.
- What do you need from me in the coming weeks? Here's what I need from you.
- What are you envisioning as your next 2-3 moves?
- What do you need most from me right now?
- What is one small brave move you need to make right now?
- What is one small brave move we need to make right now?

Deb Denbeck, President of Partnership 4 Kids, acknowledges the importance of scripting:

> **"I am pretty direct, so I need to make sure my message shows that I care about them as a person and professional. I care deeply about the people I lead, but because of my position, people sometimes fear me."**

Step 3: **Rehearse.** According to Quantified, a behavioral science organization, data shows that people are 19% less confident when they speak off the cuff. Conversations often sound better in your head than out loud, and most people are not good at speaking unrehearsed.

First, conduct a table read and note any edits or enhancements. Then stand up and practice it. Even though you will probably have the conversation while seated, standing improves your confidence. Finally, practice your script with someone you trust to provide you with honest feedback—are you coming across as caring, empathetic, clear, and concise? Heather Grato, CEO of Grato Coaching shares:

> **"Practice! With self, coach, or trusted friend. Rumor has it practice tricks the brain and nervous system, so when the actual time comes, they [the brain and nervous system] don't realize it. This makes the conversation less nerve-wracking."**

Step 4: **Plan.** Because you don't know how the other person will respond during the conversation, part of the rehearsal process is to plan for different scenarios. The following are possible reactions:

Crier: You've made your opening remarks, described the situation, and the person starts to cry. First, acknowledge the emotion:

> *"I know this is difficult for you right now."*

Second, let them know you care:

"I'm having this conversation with you because I care about you and your success."

Finally, if needed, take a break.

"Let's take a moment and see if we can continue or if we need to come back to this tomorrow."

Avoider: After you've started the conversation, the other person shuts down and you're met with silence. First, trust that silence. Give them a moment to process and formulate a response. Give them a full 10-12 seconds, which can feel like an eternity—practice keeping silent by timing it. If they haven't responded after 12 seconds, check in with them.

"What's going through your mind right now?"

"What do you think our options are in this situation?"

Deflector: A deflector will try to change the subject or inject other people into the situation. If that happens, you can redirect the conversation.

"We're here to talk about you."

"What role do you own in this situation?"

Challenger: A challenger is someone who is defensive and tries to poke holes in the situation you've presented—they challenge the facts, the message, or you directly. It could be they challenge one small detail or blame you for a part of the situation. To prevent the tendency to debate the challenges, practice for this scenario.

"Let's figure this out together."

"What does success look like to you?"

"If anything was possible, what would you do?"

Some of these are worst-case scenarios. You may have a very coachable person and the conversation goes smoothly. Either way, part of your process should always include planning and practicing so you show up at your best and can handle anything that comes your way. Jerry Kwiatkowski, Founder, Designer and Principal with Jerry Kaye Collection suggests:

"Before meeting, work through multiple responses or reactions from good to bad to be prepared for what may come. This process helps me prepare as best as

possible for any difficult questions or reactions that may come during the conversation."

During the Talk

If you have committed to the process and scripted, rehearsed, and planned your conversation, the next three steps will come more easily.

Step 1: **Manage emotions.** Hold a loose grip and do not force perfection. Stay calm, confident, and rely on the process.

Step 2: **Experiment.** Allow yourself to experiment with questions and phrases, but do so in a clear, concise way. Accept that you might stumble. It is okay to pause and say, "I didn't state that quite right. Let me try again."

Step 3: **Align.** No matter which type of tough talk you're leading, you must end with alignment and action. The other person needs to source their next steps, and you must align on when those steps will occur and in what form. Be specific and hold the other person accountable by asking them to verbally confirm.

After the Talk

Because these are tough conversations, you need to allow yourself time afterwards. The biggest mistake you can make is run to another meeting. Block time on your calendar after the conversation to process your mind, body, and energy.

Step 1: **Reflect.** How did the conversation go? How are you feeling now? What did you like about the conversation? What would you do differently? Write down these reflections.

Step 2: **Action.** What did you agree would be your next move? If the conversation wasn't successful, discuss it with someone you trust to gain clarity on your action.

Step 3: **Release.** There needs to be an energy release after the conversation. Pick a healthy way you process energy—a walk, bike ride, etc. This needs to be part of your process (more on this in chapter eight).

Without a Process

I hired a team member for my company who also happened to be a friend. She added value to the business, but I started receiving feedback from other employees that she had exhibited disruptive behavior on several occasions.

I decided to lead a Being Better conversation with her, but because we were friends, I felt I knew her well enough that I could navigate the conversation without preparation.

I opened the conversation by diving right into the situation and explaining that she had been argumentative with other team members. She immediately challenged me by questioning decisions I had made and deflected by steering the conversation to a different topic.

Despite my attempts to refocus on the situation at hand, she quickly jumped to a Moving On conversation. I assured her I only wanted her to fix her behavior, not move on from her position with the company, but she took an all or nothing stance and resigned on the spot.

The outcome was the direct result of my failure to follow a process and prepare for the conversation. I didn't bother to do any scenario planning, so I didn't anticipate her challenges. I should have paused the conversation and revisited it later, but I didn't manage my emotions, and my need to immediately solve the situation got in the way.

After the conversation, I felt horrible because my lack

of preparation made the situation worse, and despite my attempts to go back and resolve it later, our friendship was permanently damaged.

With a Process

A company's executive leadership team hired me to assess their organization and define their HR support and development needs. As the company grew through acquisitions, leadership noticed an increase in employee relations issues.

As I worked through the assessment, I discovered that one of the members of the executive leadership team was exhibiting behavioral issues. His personal development hadn't kept up with the growth of the organization and he lacked self-awareness regarding his passive-aggressive tendencies. It was now my job to lead a Being Better talk with him and share feedback he'd never heard about himself.

Before the talk

Step 1: **Prep.** I wrote down the feedback I received surrounding the situation. I was feeling hopeful that I could have an impact and help him see something he wasn't seeing. To me, that would be the ideal outcome because change could follow and I could work with him as an executive coach.

Step 2: **Script.**

1. *Conversation starter.* "The feedback I'm about to share is not good. You have a choice to either shrink or do something about it."
2. *Share the situation.* I categorized the feedback I had received into themes and included specific examples for each theme.
3. *Explore.* I wrote down questions such as, "Have you ever received this feedback before?" "How do you feel about this situation?"
4. *Align.* I assured him that everyone wanted him to be successful. "Here's how you can win, and here's how you can fail. Let's find a path forward."

Step 3: **Rehearse.** I practiced a table read of my script, made edits to areas within the feedback sections, then stood and read it aloud again.

Step 4: **Plan.** I anticipated he would be either a deflector, challenger, or possibly both, so I prepared additional statements for each scenario:

"The feedback I received is about your behavior in these situations, so we need to focus on that." "What does success look like to you in this situation?"

During the talk

Step 1: **Manage emotions.** I presented the facts surrounding the assessment I completed and outlined certain themes surrounding pillars within the organization.

When I got to the leadership pillar, I explained that I had received feedback about his own leadership style that may be difficult to hear.

Step 2: **Experiment.** I gave examples of the feedback I had received and how his leadership style was impacting the team and the organization.

He listened and asked clarifying questions, but he had a difficult time understanding how his behavior was impacting the organization.

He tried to debate some of the examples, and I restated that the information was based on the feedback I received from his direct reports and it wasn't open for debate. I also shifted the focus to opportunities for development so he could grow alongside the company.

Step 3: **Align.** I suggested two ways he could develop as a leader: through individual executive coaching and through executive education leadership development. We agreed he would reflect on our meeting and think about his next steps.

After the talk

Step 1: **Reflect.** The meeting was held at the client's location, so I reflected on the conversation during my drive home. The parts of the conversation that went well included my opening statement, my intention to present the information with warmth and energy, and using factual statements that were clear and concise.

One area I would have improved was sharing feedback from his direct reports. There was concern that if I gave specific examples, he would know who had given the feedback and retaliate against them, so I had to be vague with my examples, which made the conversation less transparent and more difficult.

Step 2: **Action.** I called the CEO to share how the conversation went and how the person and I aligned on next steps. The CEO and I scheduled a meeting with the entire executive leadership team to discuss all the findings from my assessment.

Step 3: **Release.** That evening I went for a short walk and took time to relax. I wanted to get a good night's sleep so I wouldn't carry the conversation with me into the next day.

Exceptional Results

Creating a process and following it completely is just as important as having the conversation itself. The more you prepare, practice, and process, the more confident you will become and the easier it will be. Proficiency is the goal, not perfection.

Allowing yourself to pause and pivot is part of the process. Don't forget to include the steps after the conversation. Create a process for your next brave conversation. Return to this section afterward and answer the following:

1. Did you follow all the steps for having a process?
2. Did you feel more confident going into the conversation as a result of being prepared?
3. How did the conversation compare to one when you didn't have a process?
4. Are you ready for more? Scan the QR code at the bottom of this page.

8

PROTECT YOUR ENERGY

DURING MY RECENT trip to Italy, my husband and I were scheduled to fly from Sicily to Florence with a layover in Rome. After a flight delay in Sicily, we missed our connection in Rome and couldn't catch another flight for seven hours.

This meant we'd miss the check-in window for our lodging and the plans we had made for our first evening in Florence. I hadn't anticipated this type of delay and panicked because we didn't have a plan.

My husband discovered there was a train from Rome to Florence, and the next one left in 20 minutes. I found the train app on my phone and purchased two tickets. We ran to the train station and boarded just in time. We enjoyed a relaxing two-hour ride and reached our destination within an hour of our original scheduled arrival time.

Had we taken the time to plan for delays and researched our options before traveling, we wouldn't have had to scramble at the last minute. Having strong routines and habits—such as planning what to do when you encounter travel delays—helps put you in a positive mindset so that travel is more enjoyable and unplanned disruptions are easier to manage.

Protect Your Energy

Following the process to prepare for a tough talk extends beyond scripting and practicing what you'll say. How you take care of yourself before, during, and after the conversation is key to helping you be at your best.

Protecting your energy involves setting up a routine that nourishes your body, mind, and spirit and helps manage your emotions during the process. This will ensure you are well positioned to present the message you want to deliver during the conversation and are prepared to handle unpredictability.

Think of a conversation you had when your energy was low, you were tired, or anxious. Approaching a tough talk from this perspective creates negative thoughts, such as, "What if I say the wrong thing?"

"What if they react negatively?" "What if there is awkward tension?"

You can't control how the other person reacts, but you can control how you show up to the conversation. If you show up as your best self with a positive mindset, then you will be able to embrace the uncertainty of the conversation.

Fractional CRO and Sales Coach Shannon DeSouza shares:

"Visualization and deep breathing allow me to get the clarity of the outcome I desire."

Protect Your Body

You've heard this before—nutrition, exercise, sleep, and rest are all necessary to perform at your best. If you don't protect those, then it diminishes your ability to focus your attention and have a productive conversation.

Nutrition: If you are a runner preparing for a big race, you don't eat a greasy hamburger the morning of race day. Be conscious about what you put into your body right before a tough conversation. It's also not a good idea to drink alcohol the night before. When I am hired to do a speaking engagement, I need to be at my best, so the day before, I eat healthy meals and I never drink alcohol the day before a presentation.

Exercise: Whether it's a brisk walk outside or a full workout, exercise is critical to protecting your body. I find that Tai Chi in the mornings helps me focus on what I need to accomplish. Anticipating a tough talk can make you physically tense, and exercise is a great way to release that anxiety.

Sleep: When your body is experiencing a difficult task such as a tough conversation, you need to get adequate sleep, which is 7-8 hours. Some people may be able to get by on less, but I recommend 7-8 hours the night before a tough talk to feel refreshed and at your best.

Rest: Intermittent breaks are necessary for a higher, more sustainable performance. When you rush out of a meeting right into a tough conversation and then rush to another meeting immediately after, the conversation becomes transactional. It's just another task in your day rather than an intentional conversation. It doesn't allow time for you to shift physically and mentally or process your next move.

I recommend blocking 30 minutes before you go into a tough talk to focus, center, and set your intentions. Also block 30-60 minutes immediately following the conversation to reflect, release your energy in a physical way, and then plan your next move.

Scheduled blocks of rest can feel counterintuitive to high achievers who are used to pushing through their day and moving from one task to the next.

But intermittent breaks are like the warm-up and cool-down periods for exercise. A warm-up ensures you are ready to perform, and a cool-down helps you recover. Tough conversations can take a physical toll if you aren't prepared before and after.

Protect Your Mind

Just like your body needs to be prepared to lead a tough talk, your mind needs to be ready in the form of setting your intentions. When you set your intentions, you create a new state of mind that will better serve the conversation.

Daily or weekly intention setting is a powerful technique to ensure you show up as your best self. Gail O'Bannon, Chief DEI Officer with the Dallas Mavericks says:

> **"Before having a tough conversation, I always take time to gather the facts and practice mindfulness. This allows me to**

center myself, manage my emotions, and approach the conversation with a clear, open, and informed mind."

To ready your mind for the conversation, ask yourself the following questions:

1. What do I want for this person?
2. What do I want for myself?
3. What do I want for the situation?
4. What boundaries do I need to set for this conversation, such as a time limit?
5. What is one small brave move I can make at the end of the conversation?

Write down your answers during the 30-minute time block you schedule prior to having the conversation as a way of setting your intentions and protecting your mind's energy.

When you are setting powerful intentions, you are creating within yourself a new specific mind that serves your purpose in life.

What does being my best self look like today?

Is there a relationship I want to invest in today?

One thing I can do for me today?

Are there any boundaries I want to set for myself or others today?
Could there be any conflicts I can anticipate today?

The most important thing I could accomplish today would be...

MY INTENTIONS

Build a daily or weekly habit of setting intentions. Your energy and mindset become stronger and the tough talks will flow with more ease.

Limit Distractions: For your mind to perform at its best, you also need to limit distractions. Choose a neutral place to have the conversation that is free of computers, phones, and people. If you are in a conference room, make sure it doesn't have thin or transparent walls that could allow distractions.

While you wait for the person to arrive, stay off your phone—don't check texts or emails. You may think you can multitask, but it will impact your focus. According to Harvard Business Review, a temporary shift in attention from one task to another—stopping to answer an e-mail or take a phone call, for instance—increases the amount of time necessary to finish the primary task by as much as 25%, a phenomenon known as "switching time."

Drainers: Any challenge or issue that causes you to lose focus. These are usually surprises you can't anticipate, such as a flat tire on your way to work or a sudden meeting to address a problem.

Some drainers must be dealt with immediately, but many can wait. Just because something pops up doesn't mean you have to give it your attention right away. Protect your energy by becoming good at recognizing drainers.

Fillers: Any activity that brings you joy and increases your energy. It could be a hobby, connecting with a friend, a creative activity, or sitting outside in nature. You don't have to spend a lot of time doing it, but you need fillers to increase your energy, especially before and after a tough conversation.

Protect Your Spirit

The energy you bring to the conversation becomes the spirit of that conversation. It is the reason for having the talk in the first place. Use that positive energy to look for the best possible outcome and focus on the alignment between you and the other person.

How do you want to be remembered as a leader? Do you want to be known as the leader who was brave and confident enough to have a tough conversation that was caring, clear, and concise? The impression left behind is the energy and spirit you bring to the conversation. Anne Marie Pizarro, Founder and CEO of Body Energy Connection shares:

> **"I close my eyes and take three deep, grounding breaths. Ninety-nine percent of the time I say a one sentence prayer that asks for the highest and best outcome to appear. It helps me stay calm and centered."**

Protect Your Emotions

When is your energy highest during the day? Is it first thing in the morning or late afternoon? When you feel the most positive is the time of day you should lead a tough conversation. You don't lead as effectively during the times when your energy is low. You can easily slip into negative emotions, especially when drainers pop up.

The How We Work talk is a great way to ask those you work with what time of day they have the most positive energy. That way if you ever need to lead a tough talk with them, chances are it will be more successful if you hold it during the time when their emotions are most positive.

To help protect your emotions before a tough talk, there are several helpful habits you can practice:

1. *Positive statements.* Write down positive "what if" statements to refocus your frame of mind. "What if they receive the feedback well?" "What if they seek to understand and explore opportunities?" "What if we quickly align on next steps?"
2. *Practice gratitude.* Show positive emotion toward someone else. For example, send an email letting someone know they did a good

job in a meeting or presentation, or write a note thanking someone for their help on a project. Gratitude is the fastest way to put yourself into a positive mindset.

3. *Face your fears.* Focus on progress over perfection. No tough talk will ever go perfectly, but the fact you are brave enough to have it will advance progress. Don't worry about being perfect. Instead, visualize the ideal outcome and then work to get there.

4. *Deep breathing.* If you feel anxious before the conversation, inhale slowly for 5 seconds and then exhale slowly for 5 seconds. This can turn off the fight or flight response and reset your emotions to focus on a positive outcome.

If none of these habits work, seek out a trusted person and talk through your emotions so you can enter the conversation with a positive perspective. It will also help you manage your emotions during the conversation, especially if you need to explore deeper or pivot.

Protecting My Energy

When I practice managing my body, mind, spirit, and emotions, I go into a tough conversation with confidence, I'm exploratory, and I'm outcome driven. The times when I haven't followed these practices, I'm hesitant, unclear, my voice quivers, and I shut down.

Protecting my energy before, during, and after the tough conversation with the member of the executive leadership team I described in chapter seven required several days of planning.

Body: I went to bed early multiple nights in a row. I practiced Tai Chi every morning. I also tried to have healthier meals.

Mind: I checked my calendar to ensure I had scheduled time for fillers and that there weren't any potential drainers, such as meetings that could wait until later. I also blocked 30 minutes immediately before the conversation to breathe, relax, and get my stomach butterflies into formation. I turned off all devices, read my notes, and centered myself. After the conversation, I blocked another 30 minutes to reflect and reach out to the CEO to discuss next steps.

Spirit: I set my intentions for the conversation, which included for him to hear my message and seek to understand and learn ways he could drive positive action.

Emotions: I was nervous about his reaction during the conversation, but I focused on the positive outcome I wanted. I reminded myself I didn't have to be perfect

—I just needed to deliver the feedback in a clear and caring way so he could take action.

Here are additional energy practices you can try:

ENERGY AND MINDSET PRACTICES

When you **do not** think, say, or act in your true, authentic self, your blue chakra may get blocked. The inability to communicate effectively and an overall sensation of incompetence are two typical signs of throat chakra imbalance. That is why your neck constricts when you are nervous or agitated, and you have a blockage in your throat as you attempt to contain your emotions.

Practice these...

Heal with your voice by:

Speaking
Humming
Singing
Laughing
Shouting
Saying Mantras

Hearing & Sound Remedy:

Vocal toning
Drumming
Tuning Forks
Gongs
Windchimes
Singing Bowls

Affirmations:
Say To Yourself

I am forthright and truthful in my conversation.

I am capable of having a tough conversation.

I'm expressing myself clearly and confidently.

I trust I can do this.
.....

Crystals:
How To Use Blue Lace Agate

The stone of communication, making it easier to feel confident and communicate.

Place in your office to aid with effective communication between people.

You can carry it in your pocket if you have to speak or perform in public.

Neck Exercises:

Upper Trapezius Stretch
Neck Rolls
Neck Rotation
Neck Stretches

Breathing Exercises:

Tai Chi
or
One deep breath, followed by three deep double breaths

Exceptional Results

When you focus on what is in your control and do so with positive, intentional actions, you can protect your energy and show up as the best version of yourself. This is a big part of what makes tough talks easier to lead and end in exceptional results. After leading your next brave conversation, return to this section and answer the following:

1. How did you protect your energy before the conversation?
2. How did you protect your energy following the conversation?
3. Did you include fillers?
4. What drainers popped up and did you limit them?
5. Are you ready for more? Scan the QR code at the bottom of this page.

9

LEADING BRAVE CONVERSATIONS

ONE OF THE biggest barriers to leading a tough talk is fear, especially the fear of how the other person will respond. Rather than focus on that fear and what you can't control, focus on what you *can* control—how you show up to the conversation. Proper preparation is the best way to overcome your fear.

In chapter seven, I discussed the process for leading a tough talk. In this chapter, I'm going to dive deeper into the part of the process before the conversation: prep, script, rehearse, and plan. I want you to have a step-by-step guide for how to prepare so you can deliver your message in a clear, concise way and end with action that leads to exceptional results.

Some people may think they don't need to script and rehearse a tough talk—they feel they do just fine speaking off the cuff. This may be true in some circumstances, but scripting and rehearsing is the only way to check if your message is clear and concise.

Jotting down a few bullet points on paper right before the talk may seem sufficient, but more than likely you will do nothing more than repeat those few points over and over during the conversation.

The result is an awkward, uncomfortable exchange that impacts your confidence. Preparation—being intentional about the message, words, and tone of your voice—shows the other person that you take the situation seriously and want the conversation to be impactful.

I was hired by a company to help plan a company-wide reorganization, followed by leadership development. We moved from individual business units to a single unit, which required leaders to interact differently. To kick off the session, both the CEO and chief administrative officer (CAO) spoke to the group.

The CEO walked into the room and placed two props on each table—peanut butter Pop-Tarts® and a can of WD-40. He used the props to illustrate the difference between what happens when you have a leadership team that helps drives change (Kellogg's innovation of peanut butter Pop-Tarts®) and a leadership team that doesn't push themselves outside of their comfort zone

(WD-40). The CEO had clearly prepared and thought through his message and performance, which was delivered clearly, concisely, and was well received.

When the CAO spoke, he read directly from a piece of paper with a few notes he had scribbled moments before he walked into the room. His message fell flat.

Afterward, he asked me how I thought he'd done. I pointed out the differences between his presentation and the CEO's. He realized his lack of preparation had hurt his opportunity to deliver a powerful message like the CEO had done.

When I started my consulting business, I never scripted my introductions—I left that up to the leader. Prior to one of the introductions, the HR manager assured me that their CEO would give me a wonderful introduction that would be powerful in setting the tone for the session.

When the CEO introduced me, he said, "This is Nicole. She's going to be our trainer for the day because she won the bid." I was mortified—not only did he incorrectly refer to me as a "trainer" rather than as an "executive coach," but the only qualification he used was that I had won the bid. I learned my lesson and now fully script my own introductions for others to deliver.

Prior to every speaking engagement, I prep, script,

rehearse, and plan. Scripting and rehearsing are the most important parts. I script everything I'm going to say and then I practice. I pay attention to operative words to help communicate meaning, I use contrasting ideas, and I incorporate storytelling to drive home my points.

I also work on my performance—posture, how I use my hands, and my voice. I pay attention to my movements and don't wander back and forth across the stage.

When having a tough talk, scripting and rehearsing help you deliver a powerful message that builds your confidence, making it easier to have the conversations when needed. *How* you are going to say it is just as important as *what* you are going to say.

How to Prepare

Now that you understand *why* you must prepare for a tough talk, I will teach you *how* to prepare. There are seven steps to follow before every conversation:

1. Pause and think. This will help drive your message toward clarity. You have probably felt frustrated with the situation and fearful of the conversation, so acknowledging your emotions will help you look at the situation from all angles. Don't skip this step—use these questions from chapter seven as a way to bring focus to your conversation.

PAUSE AND THINK

What are the facts of the situation?

How do you feel about the situation at this moment - surprise, fear, anger, sadness, or frustration?

What is the desired outcome for you and for the other person?

What is important for you to let them know?

What are you most curious about? List 2-3 questions.

What part of the situation do you own—did something slip through the cracks? Was a promise not fulfilled? Did you have competing priorities?

How urgent is this situation—does it need to be address today, tomorrow, or within the next week?

2. **Script.** Crafting your message points is another way to be intentional with the conversation.

DRAFT THE SCRIPT

A conversation starter, remember clear and kind. (Reference each chapter for conversation starters)

Share up to three facts of the situation

Explore with a powerful question and pause... trust silence.

Can you share what might be happening?
I want to hear how you are viewing the situation...
Talk to me about what's going on...

Ask another question to understand the situation - stay curious...

Pause and take a moment to summarize and align.
Let's make sure we are on the same page...
Here is what I am hearing...

Ask a question for action:
What is one move you can make right now?
What is one thing you want to focus on?

Ending with action + accountability:
Let's summarize what we (you) have agreed to...
When can we check in?

---

*Nicole***Bianchi**
WWW.NICOLEMBIANCHI.COM

---

3. Detailed script. If you need more details and want to write out your entire script, you can use the following:

TOUGH TALK WORKSHEET

Conversation Starter

Facts:
1.
2.
3.

Explore with a powerful question and pause... trust silence.

Ask another question to understand the situation - stay curious...

Pause and take a moment to summarize and align.

Ask a question for action:

Ending with action and accountability:

You've done the work.
You've got this!
Remember, one small brave move at a time.

---

4. Table read. Don't simply review the message in your head. Verbalize it by reading your script out loud while seated. This will help you edit and enhance your script for clarity. Pay attention to the following:

Pace of speech—don't rush through your message.

Tone, volume, and inflection of your voice.

Word choice—use "and" instead of "but;" don't say "always" or "never;" don't say "it's not personal."

Don't suggest solutions to the problem—the other person needs to source their own action.

Reminder—don't use the feedback sandwich.

5. Practice. If possible, find someone to practice with in person. This is especially helpful for the tougher talks so you can become comfortable with off-script moments during the conversation. A practice partner can confirm if the message is clear and concise, if your style, words, and tempo are appropriate, and help you practice scenarios.

If you anticipate the tough talk will be with a person who is a deflector or challenger, give your practice partner background information and ask them to present difficult responses. This will allow you to ask the exploration questions you've prepared in your script to seek understanding and alignment.

Your practice partner can also suggest three things to continue doing and two things to consider changing with your script.

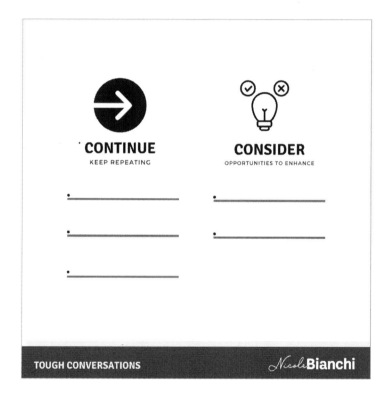

6. **Perform.** After the table read and making edits and enhancements, stand up and practice again. This

helps build your confidence, ensure your script is polished, and gives you the opportunity to add any finishing touches.

7. Logistics. You must also prepare the details of the conversation such as location, time of day, and blocking your calendar before and after. Revisit chapter eight to ensure you protect your energy—body, mind, spirit, and emotions—as part of the preparation process.

Exceptional Results

The best way to make a tough talk easier is with proper preparation. Set your intentions for the conversation and script your message so it is clear and concise.

You will increase your confidence the more you prepare—you got this! After leading your next brave conversation, return to this section and answer the following:

1. How did you feel before preparing for the conversation?
2. What edits and enhancements did you make to your script?
3. Did you practice with a partner?
4. Did you feel more confident going into the conversation?

5. Are you ready for more? Scan the QR code at the bottom of this page.

CONCLUSION

Tough talks are more difficult when you avoid them. Now that you understand each type, why you must have them, when to have them, and most importantly, how to have them, you can turn the five tough talks into five brave conversations. All it takes is preparation. The more you prepare, the greater your confidence.

Remember: bravery is a skill, and leadership is an action. Let this be your playbook to teach you the skills needed to become a better leader who achieves exceptional results.

Judi Holler, speaker, author, and founder of Holla! Worldwide, says:

> **"I don't know many people who like confrontation or tough conversations, but**

getting in uncomfortable situations is a leadership skill that must be mastered if you want to stay in business. These days I look at every tough conversation as a muscle I am building to keep my business strong."

Anyone can lead a brave conversation. The best leaders recognize the value in having team members who can resolve conflict among themselves instead of bringing every issue to the leader. Teaching an entire team how to lead tough talks is a game changer within an organization.

Facilitating your team through a How We Work conversation sets the foundation so they can quickly recognize if they need to have The Ask or What's Going On? talk with you or one of their peers. It keeps everyone aligned, eliminating the frequency of the two toughest talks.

Michael Bungay Stanier shares:

> **"Before you jump into the what, have a conversation about how we work together because that conversation actually gives permission to keep talking about the health of the relationship, and an ability to keep revisiting the health of the rela-**

tionship gives the relationship a chance to be healthy."

We teach leaders and their teams how to have the five tough talks to drive peer accountability. We also facilitate one-on-one and executive team coaching, conduct half and full-day workshops, and serve as keynote speakers to entire organizations on leading brave conversations.

Here are comments from some of our clients:

Speaking

> "She is very engaging, energetic and inspiring! I like it when she said, "What is the worst thing that could happen" if I did this? I am definitely going to ask myself this question when I am afraid to try something new."

> "She is hilarious. Her message is very valuable and needed to hear. Not just to build confidence but to also strengthen your skill set as a leader. She's very engaging and makes you feel comfortable. I love everything about her session."

> "Nicole was inspiring, fun and interesting. Her topic of being brave is relatable and she makes very great points of breaking out of comfort zones."

Writing

"Bianchi's contribution to the field of leadership lies in her ability to simplify acts of bravery, making them accessible and doable for all of us—one small step at a time. She then breathes life into these small acts through wonderful story telling. [*Small Brave Moves*] is a book well worth reading if you want to strengthen your bravery muscles as a leader!" *Pam McLean, Ph.D., Author, Self as Coach, Self as Leader*

"Nicole writes from experience and the heart. Her wisdom and personal stories give her readers perspective and hope for the future. This book [*Small Brave Moves*] is for every man, woman, and child—it's a personal, practical guide for living in the real world as leaders. Through little acts of bravery we can all change the way we live inside our stories." *Tasha Wahl, Founder and Chief Executive Officer, The Butterfly Effect*

"One day, one moment at a time, we all have the capacity for Bravership! Each day is an opportunity to show up as our best selves. *Small Brave Moves* is a great reminder to reflect, embrace our strengths, and push ourselves to new limits!" *Dana Vollmer, 5-time Olympic Gold Medalist*

Coaching

"Nicole is masterful at asking powerful questions to really think about the challenge I am facing and the next move I need to make."

"Nicole has become my go-to thought partner on navigating difficult choices and challenges. Having a coach has been a game-changer for me."

"She shows she really cares and wants to dig into the root of a situation and how I could be a better leader out of it while introducing new tools and holding me accountable for action."

After you have led a few brave conversations and feel more confident in your ability, come back and retake the self-assessment that you took in chapter one:

Rate yourself on FREQUENCY:

How frequently do you have these tough talks?

1 Never
2 Rarely
3 Sometimes
4 Usually
5 Always

TOUGH TALK TYPE	FREQUENCY
MOVING ON	
BEING BETTER	
WHAT'S GOING ON?	
THE ASK	
HOW WE WORK	

Rate yourself on CONFIDENCE:

How confident are you in having these tough talks?

1 Not confident
2 Slightly
3 Somewhat
4 Fairly
5 Very confident

TOUGH TALK TYPE	CONFIDENCE
MOVING ON	
BEING BETTER	
WHAT'S GOING ON?	
THE ASK	
HOW WE WORK	

The result of the self-assessment will prove that when you prepare, practice, and perform one tough talk and then another, confidence replaces fear. This confidence increases the frequency of the first three conversation types and decreases the last two. The bravery you exhibit will lead you, your team, and your organization to exceptional results.

FIRST, IT IS AN INTENTION

THEN A BEHAVIOR

THEN A HABIT

THEN A PRACTICE

THEN SECOND NATURE

THEN IT IS SIMPLY WHO YOU ARE

WWW.NICOLEMBIANCHI.COM

YOU DON'T HAVE TO GO IT ALONE

If you have made it to the end of this book, you are ready to go have a tough conversation or two. Take a moment. There is much more inside of you than you know. Give yourself a high five, cue the confetti, and choose your favorite song as walk-in music—it's a moment to celebrate!

Ready for More?

Here are a few ways to stay connected and work with me and our team.

1. **Sign up for my newsletter.** My newsletter is a fan favorite. I share three things I am working on, including actionable tools for you to be a bit braver in

the work you are doing. Sign up on my site: nicolembianchi.com

2. **Follow me on social media.** I share tools, resources, and ideas to help you.

3. **Hire me to speak at your next retreat, conference, or company meeting.** I offer inspiring and actionable keynote speeches, executive coaching, and workshops designed to help you and your teams craft their own small brave moves or have their own tough conversations.

4. **Bring Tough Talks to your workplace.** Our workshops, 1:1 coaching, and certifications enable you to build capabilities in house.

Scan this QR code to access all the tools listed above. Add me to your circle. Let's be friends. Forever. (Don't make it weird.)

Will You Help?

Amazon reviews are trusted more than any other type of review and serve as a catalyst for more sales. Would you please leave an honest Amazon review? I appreciate you!

SELECTED REFERENCES

Chapter One
The Five Types of Tough Talks

Klaver, M. Nora. 2007. *Mayday! Asking for Help in Times of Need.* Berrett-Koehler Publishers.

Coyle, Daniel. 2018. *The Culture Code: The Secrets of Highly Successful Groups.* Bantam.

Fay, Dr. Charles. 2022. "Modeling Healthy Relationships." *loveandlogic.com.* July 21. https://www.loveandlogic.com/blogs/our-blog/modeling-healthy-relationships.

Maxfield, Brittney. 2019. "Office Haunting: 8 out of 10 employees are running in fear from a scary conversation at work." *Crucial-learning.com.* October 3.

Ferriss, Timothy. 2017. *Tribe of Mentors: Short Life Advice from the Best in the World.* Harper Business.

Chapter Two
How We Work

Franco, Samantha. 2022. "The Real Reason For Van Halen's Infamous 'NO BROWN M&Ms' Concert Venue Request." *https://www.thevintagenews.com/2022/07/22/cabrini-green/?D5c=1&A5c=1&D_4_6cALL=1&D_4_6_10cALL=1.* July 25.

Chapter Three
The Ask

Melore, Chris. 2022. "Stubborn Nation: 3 in 4 people don't ask for help until they absolutely need it." *studyfinds.org*. January 20. https://studyfinds.org/stubborn-nation-asking-for-help/.

Chapter Five
Being Better

n.d. "Use Situation-Behavior-Impact™ (SBI) to Understand Intent." *ccl.org*. https://www.ccl.org/articles/leading-effec tively-articles/closing-the-gap-between-intent-vs-impact-sbii.

Chapter Six
Moving On

2019. "New DDI Research: 57 Percent of Employees Quit Because of Their Boss." PR Newswire, December 9.

Chapter Seven
The Tough Talk Process

2016. "Why are Speakers 19% Less Confident in Impromptu Settings?" https://www.quantified.ai/blog/why-are-speakers-19-less-confident-in-impromptu-settings/

Chapter Eight
Protect Your Energy

McCarthy, Tony Schwartz and Catherine. 2007. "Manage Your Energy, Not Your Time." *Harvard Business Review*. https://hbr.

org/2007/10/manage-your-energy-not-your-time#:~:text=Dis-
tractions%20are%20costly%3A%20A%20tempo-
rary,known%20as%20%E2%80%9Cswitching%20time.%E2%80%9D

ACKNOWLEDGMENTS

Thank you to my husband, best friend, and love of my life, Dave, for planting the seed for a beautiful journey in Italy for almost seven weeks, allowing me to break away from my business and life to write and develop the framework for *Five Tough Talks*. Every single pivotal moment in my life is because of you.

To my daughter, Moe, you are learning tough conversations at an age where I wish I had this skill. I see your confidence building each and every time. You are a strong and beautiful woman who is leaving her mark. I am proud of how you move through this world every single day. I can't wait for your next chapter to unfold. I love you without end.

To my son, Joe, my best looking, most skilled, the "Swiss army knife" of the three, and the most charming child. If you are reading this, please laugh with me, Nicole, for just a moment. (Joe added this little bit into my Acknowledgements while I was having him review something else. Now it is my turn to say a little something.) Joe, you light up the room when you walk in, and you aren't afraid to say what needs to be said. You have a strong reputation for being smart, hard-working, and coachable, and it will take you so far in this world. You make me proud off the field and on. Always know I love you so much more.

To my son, Nic, you began learning tough conversations in 5th grade when you fired your first salesperson for poor performance, just before starting Bianchi Candle Co. You have a huge heart and that can make tough conversations even tougher. I love watching you grow as a leader while watching you grow your business. I am thankful we have each other to lean on in business and life. I love you 135.999.

Being introduced to you, Kathy Rygg, has been one of my happiest moments! Finding you to partner with to help bring a concept, framework, stories, and ideas to life. You complete me, and I deeply appreciate you! Thank you, Kelly Laine Design, for bringing just a concept to life in the most incredible visual way. You are talented beyond measure.

The book is the evolution of many executive coaching conversations and tough conversations workshops with leaders all over the world. It is clear, it doesn't matter where we are in our leadership journey, tough conversations continue to be just that—tough.

It is rare for an author to get the opportunity to proto-type and experiment with concepts with their clients through coaching and workshops. I am so grateful for clients who say YES and trust me through the entire process. A special thank you to Denice Biocca and the global HR team at GE Gas and Power; Amy Birkel and the Heritage Communities Leadership team; Phillip James, Chris Vansickle, and the WEG Leader-ship team, Percy Fields and the Belt Railway Leader-ship team, Chris Mehaffey and the Mid-America Boy Scouts Council Leadership team; and Donna Kush with the Omaha Community Foundation Leadership team.

To all of the incredible authors and thought leaders mentioned in this book, thank you for saying yes!

To everyone on my team—yesterday, today, and tomor-row. You are changing the world with me, one conver-sation at a time! A special thank you to Shannon Desouza, Sam Vetter, Sarah Huguet, Sophie Armstrong, Amber Giangregorio, and Pam Rocholz.

To my speaker thought partners: Shawna Suckow, Kim Becking, Justin Patton, Anne Bonney, and Pat Dwyer. Thank you for always shooting it to me straight, no chaser. I trust you and am so thankful for you!

In the middle of writing my book, I was working on the conversations in the Lionshead Irish Pub in Florence, Italy, when Niccolò Fortini and a colleague of his asked to join my husband's and my table. The place was packed as Fiorentino was about to play their neighboring rival Bologna. I remember in the moment I was going to use time during the game to write out some more stories when I realized a story was about to unfold.

We spent two hours laughing, cheering, and learning so much more about the sport and each other. Before we said our goodbyes, Niccolò said to us, "This right here is so important: face-to-face conversation. Being with people, understanding people, and showing kindness to each other." Niccolò reminded me of the importance of being in the moment and building relationships.

ABOUT THE AUTHOR

Award-winning entrepreneur Nicole Bianchi is the ultimate success story. From life on a farm to 16 years in leadership roles in two Fortune 300 companies, Bianchi learned on the job what it truly takes to be a great leader. Through what she describes as true bravery through consistent small moves, Bianchi founded her own company in 2012, and her passion for helping others led her to coaching, consulting, and to penning her first book *Small Brave Moves*. Known for coining the term "Bravership" and widely regarded as the go-to source for bravery and leadership, Nicole now serves as a consultant, master coach, and transformational speaker who has partnered with brands all over the globe.

Her passion? Inspiring Bravery.

Her focus? Enabling leaders to stretch into their bravest selves.

"Nicole Bianchi cuts through the noise and delivers a clear, concise, and important message. Bravership, a term coined and trademarked by Bianchi, is written as a reminder on the walls of c-suite executives across North America. What makes her different? Her message is bravery, and she makes it accessible to all"- *Mentors Collective Magazine*.

When she's not busy writing books, hosting retreats around the globe, or speaking on international stages, Bianchi loves traveling with her husband and cheering on her three children in life. You can catch her singing off-key karaoke with a full-bodied glass of wine in hand! Visit her at https://www.nicolembianchi.com.

Made in the USA
Columbia, SC
27 January 2025

78f553bc-b906-4b18-a5b3-b237cc4ecfe1R01